Parenting Toddlers

Toddler Discipline Tips and Tricks for Happy Kids

(The Ultimate Guide to Using Positive Discipline to Raise Children)

Robert Velazquez

Published by Rob Miles

© **Robert Velazquez**

All Rights Reserved

Parenting Toddlers: Toddler Discipline Tips and Tricks for Happy Kids (The Ultimate Guide to Using Positive Discipline to Raise Children)

ISBN 9781990084454

All rights reserved. No part of this guide may be reproduced in any form without permission in writing from the publisher except in the case of brief quotations embodied in critical articles or reviews.

Legal & Disclaimer

The information contained in this book is not designed to replace or take the place of any form of medicine or professional medical advice. The information in this book has been provided for educational and entertainment purposes only.

The information contained in this book has been compiled from sources deemed reliable, and it is accurate to the best of the Author's knowledge; however, the Author cannot guarantee its accuracy and validity and cannot be held liable for any errors or omissions. Changes are periodically made to this book. You must consult your doctor or get professional medical advice before using any of the suggested remedies, techniques, or information in this book.

Upon using the information contained in this book, you agree to hold harmless the Author from and against any damages, costs, and expenses, including any legal fees potentially resulting from the application of any of the information provided by this guide. This disclaimer applies to any damages or injury caused by the use and application, whether directly or indirectly, of any advice or information presented, whether for breach of contract, tort, negligence, personal injury, criminal intent, or under any other cause of action.

You agree to accept all risks of using the information presented inside this book. You need to consult a professional medical practitioner in order to ensure you are both able and healthy enough to participate in this program.

Table of Contents

INTRODUCTION 1

CHAPTER 1: SIGNIFICANCE OF DEVELOPING A SUCCESS MINDSET IN CHILDREN 3

CHAPTER 2: GRAB HOLD OF THE REINS 7

CHAPTER 3: IT TAKES A VILLAGE 11

CHAPTER 4: EXPLAINING DIVORCE TO YOUR KIDS 19

CHAPTER 5: WHAT IS THE REASON FOR TEACHING CHILDREN ENTREPRENEURSHIP? WHY IS IT IMPORTANT? 24

CHAPTER 6: SPEND TIME WITH CHILDREN 33

CHAPTER 7: TEACHING KIDS RESPONSIBILITY 36

CHAPTER 8: CONNECTING ON OUR CHILD'S LEVEL 41

CHAPTER 9: TOP COMMON SINGLE PARENT FEARS 51

CHAPTER 10: THE CONSISTENT PARENT 55

CHAPTER 11: YOUR CHILD AND YOUR LOVE LIFE 59

CHAPTER 12: HERE IS HOW IT WORKS: 65

CHAPTER 12: TODDLER PROOFING YOUR HOUSE 73

CHAPTER 13: THE FIVE TYPES OF EX-SPOUSE RELATIONSHIPS 82

CHAPTER 14: ESSENTIAL LESSONS ON EMOTIONAL SKILLS 96

CHAPTER 15: POSITIVE DISCIPLINE 100

CHAPTER 16	104
CHAPTER 17: DEALING WITH PUBLIC TANTRUMS	112
CHAPTER 18: PREVENTIONS & SOLUTIONS	119
CHAPTER 19: THE CONTRIBUTIONS OF DAD	132
CHAPTER 20: HOW TO GET MORE INVOLVED IN YOUR CHILD'S EDUCATION	136
CHAPTER 21: GET ACTIVE	146
CHAPTER 22: USE SUPPLEMENTS TO MAINTAIN YOUR CHILDREN'S HEALTH NATURALLY	152
CHAPTER 23: HOW TO TALK TO YOUR TEEN	157
CHAPTER 24: WHAT NOT TO DO AND WHY	164
CHAPTER 25: HOW TO PRAISE YOUR TODDLER THE RIGHT WAY	168
CHAPTER 26: TECHNO TEEN	174
CHAPTER 27: HOW TO ENSURE YOUR CHILD MAKES GOOD CHOICES	181
CHAPTER 28: COMMON PITFALLS AND TRAPS	184
CHAPTER 29: BECOME A GREAT STEPFATHER	191
CHAPTER 30: SMART KIDS ARE RESILIENT	196
CONCLUSION	201

Introduction

Kids.As cliché as it may sound, they really are the future.No kids, no human race, no human future.And as a parent, or someone who is considering the possibility, it is your job to raise your own little people to become good, honest adults who are capable of raising families of their own.A little slice of the future is literally in your hands.No pressure.

If you have found this small book, you are already all-too familiar with the fact that there are literally hundreds of books out there that profess to have the perfect parenting method all laid out.All you need to do is follow each chapter step by step and one day your little boy or girl will be a Fortune 500 CEO, tennis star or the President.

Every meal is planned, extracurricular activity scheduled and odd personality trait is analyzed.So, what does this book have to offer that hasn't already been put out by the Dr. Spocks, Drews, Ozs and Phils of the world?The answer is simple, here you will find advice from a real father with real kids living in the real world.

Is my situation exactly like yours?Probably not.But that doesn't matter.This isn't a how-to book.It is a collection of simple advice and observations that come from raising kids in the modern world. Most people will be able to find at least something in these pages that applies.

Instead of checklists, we'll spend time going over things like what your expectations should (and should not be), certain basic things that every parent should do, and how you can help your child grow into who he is meant to be.

Now, let's get started.

Chapter 1: Significance Of Developing A

Success Mindset In Children

Before moving on to the different strategies and tactics needed to help cultivate and unleash the growth mindset in your child, let's start by understanding the need to develop a growth mindset in your child/children.

If your child believes in him or herself, he or she can accomplish anything he or she focuses on. In addition, there are numerous reasons why developing a growth mindset in your children is important; below are a few of these:

It helps your child realize his or her hidden talents: At birth, all of us have some innate unique talents. Your child is no different; he or she has unique ability and talents. If you do not help your child realize these talents and abilities, he or she may end up having a career or life he or she despises. The child may be bored and exhausted with his or her life because he or she would not be doing what he or she was meant to do.

On the other hand, if you help your child develop a growth and success mindset now, he or she will recognize their capabilities, which with persistence and hard work, can be refined into enjoyable lifelong careers. This discovery will help your child do something he or she enjoys, and form meaningful life goals.

Helps develop self-confidence: A positive frame of mind helps instill self-confidence. When a child is confident, he or she understands that he or she is capable of whatever they focus on.

However, if you fail to work on finding out the type of thoughts brewing in your child's mind, and what mindset is developing within him or her, you would never be able to know whether your child has confidence issues. It is likely your child will gravitate towards negative thinking; negative thinking shatters confidence, preventing your child from doing anything meaningful in life.

If you don't want that to happen to your bundle of joy, you must work on developing a growth mindset in your children.

Helps embrace their uniqueness: In addition to helping your child recognize his or her inner power/strengths, and developing self-assurance, a growth mindset gives your child the strength needed to embrace his or her uniqueness.

It helps your child know that he or she is great the way he or she is, and should not be shy of his or her individuality. This helps your child to grow into a strong, mature, and courageous individual who is ready to battle every struggle life throws their way.

Unlock creativity: By helping your child develop a positive frame of mind, you help him or her think out of the box and stay hopeful irrespective of how dire a situation seems.

By unlocking your child's creative power, you help the child come up with unique ideas that empower him or her to resolve difficulties. When your child is innovative, you need not worry about his or her success because his or her creative ideas will certainly help the child objectify his or her goals.

The above benefits should have served to cement the need to develop the right mindset in your child. Without further ado, let us look at how to develop the growth mindset in your child.

Chapter 2: Grab Hold Of The Reins

Sometimes it can be pretty easy to lose it when your child is throwing a fit. Some parents don't realize that they do it almost automatically. It's easy to be angry when someone else is angry. Sometimes we feel that we are justified in our actions simply because we were provoked by someone else.

But that is not the case with a tantrum. As stated earlier in the previous chapter, toddlers will throw a tantrum for various reasons. Most of the time, they do it just to get what they want. At times they are just venting out their frustrations and sadness.

Don't Mirror the Stress: Show Some Sympathy and Empathize

Do you tend to get angry and frustrated too when your child loses it? What do you do when your child throws a tantrum? Understanding where your child is coming from – empathizing – actually helps you stop yourself from throwing a fit yourself. Try not to lose it when your child loses it.

Remember that when your kid throws a fit, he or she is the one with the problem – not you. They're frustrated, they're angry, and if you join in then it only feeds the stressful situation. You eventually end up stressed, both child and parents only end up getting stressed when everyone pitches in the tantrum parade.

As a parent it is also your job to make sure that your children are in a safe place when they throw a tantrum. Remember that they can do a lot of crazy things that can eventually hurt themselves. Take time to calm yourself before you deal with your child's emotions.

Don't expect to be able to calm your child when you yourself are having an anxiety attack. Take deep breaths and make sure that you are calm, reassuring, caring, and ready to take on the role of mommy or daddy. If you're too stressed out to handle the situation then call on your partner or spouse and let them handle it. Don't try to patch things up when you're too emotionally engrossed in the situation — you may not be the best person to help your child cope at the moment.

Take Time to Deal with Your Own Emotions and Frustrations

If you find yourself too stressed out and unable to deal with your toddler's meltdowns then take a timeout. Talk to someone about your feelings. Take the time to vent. Talk to your spouse or partner and express your frustrations. You should find a way to let it out when emotions are just too high.

You should also make sure to make time for yourself. Try to do something that calms you. Sometimes all it takes is a relaxing warm bath. Some parents order some pizza or any of their favorite comfort foods (of course you have to watch the calories too).

Another way to blow off steam is to do some exercise. Remember that anger is an emotion of action. It makes you want to do something and fast. Sometimes the solution is not to remove the thing that is causing the irritation or anger. Sometimes all takes is to get some quiet time.

Once you are calm and relaxed don't go to your child just yet. Remind yourself that your child's ability to express himself or herself is really limited. Remember that a toddler just can't cope with all the different situations he or she encounters. They can't express their thoughts and emotions clearly.

Once you have your own emotions in check it is time to face your child's tantrum. You need to be the parent that your child can look up to. You need to be calm and in control not freaking out with them.

Chapter 3: It Takes A Village

I grew up with a girl named Heather.Now, I do not want to say that her mother was not a good cook, for I enjoyed many delicious meals that she prepared.However, cooking was not her mother's first love and her repertoire was good, but limited.On the other hand, my mother always had a way of putting a meal together and could have (should have) filled a recipe book with her diverse kitchen experience.Heather learned from my mom how to cook a wider diversity of delectable items and had her health not failed her, she might have out done my mother in terms of good, old-fashioned hospitality.

Her parents had a dramatic effect on who I am today as well.The time I spent in their house proved instrumental in many of the attributes I have been privileged to carry into manhood.**It takes a village**.Your family unit was never intended to exist as if on an island.You need other people in the process.Other parents need you in the process.The 'village' is an integral part of a child's development.

Many times, when we look at generations past, we ignorantly point to mother's being home as the sole reason why children appear to have been raised more effectively.However, when you realize the simple aspects of an agrarian society, that circle of positive influence expands rapidly.For instance, in a farm setting, the children would come home from school, have lunch with mom and then proceed to help their father in the fields for as long as daylight held.With dad working along side his children, he played a critical role in their day-to-day development.

But the influence did not stop with Dad.Often, farms were family conglomerates.Aunts, Uncles, Cousins and Grandparents would be right with your children as they performed their chores.Neighbors might help with harvest, again expanding the circle of influence.The family might, in turn, help the neighbors with their harvest as well.In other words, the entire community would have some direct level of influence in the life of each and every child.

The best example of this I could give you in modern times was Nellie Olsen from the well-known seventies television series, Little House on the Prairie.The golden-locked character was a certified brat- Old West style.Her mother thought she could do no wrong.Her father cow-toed to everything she and her mother did.They owned the general store in Walnut Grove, which certified that Nellie and her brother were a bit on the spoiled side.Yet the writers of this iconic show realized that all the times the kids and adults of Walnut Grove stood up to Nellie, their actions had a direct effect on the girl.So, when she finally reached adulthood, we found a woman with a more tempered temperament.In fact, Nellie, as a young woman, proved to be rather pleasant.

Having said that, there is another common theme in early twentieth century literature when it comes to the small town.The late twentieth century produced the idea of 'cocooning.'The most common sign of this phenomenon is the automatically closing garage doors that dominate our suburban landscape.We disappear into our castles and rarely know who our neighbors are.But we are families, right?'Cocooning' as a nuclear family is what it takes these days... doesn't it?

Yet when we read stories from the early part of the last century, those that 'cocooned' were considered a detriment- even a danger- to the community.Consider the Radley House from, To Kill a Mockingbird (Harper Lee; 1960).Though Boo Radley turns out a hero in the end of the book, the house and its inhabitants are met with much skepticism and mistrust, if not with a level of loathing.People knew each other.To not be known in the community was a dark mark on a family or individual.**In the early part of the century, only those who were not considered productive in society disappeared into their houses at night, rarely to be seen.**My, how times have changed.

The Hawaiians present us with a perfect word for what our children need. That word is 'Mahalo.' Mahalo is not just family, but the idea that the 'village' is family. I grew up with the understanding that Heather's family was as much my uncle, aunt and cousins as my own uncle, aunt and cousins. It is this mentality that led to my success as an adult. Debbie and Rodney (Heather's parents) and a host of other friends of my parents played critical roles in this boy becoming a man. If you are to raise children to become the men and women they need to be, then your children don't just need their own uncles, aunts and cousins, they need 'village' uncles, aunts and cousins as well.

Do you know how to make ugly rocks become beautiful, shiny stones? You put them in a rock tumbler. In the tumbler, the rocks bang into each other, knock off all the rough edges each stone has, leaving, at the conclusion of the process, smooth, shiny, beautiful stones. Our 'village' that we are talking about is the proverbial rock tumbler our children need. Having other people around them with other rough, emotional edges presents the opportunity for each person to be smoothed in- and by- the process.That guy from work who claims to have a mild allergy to children might just help your children realize that some people in the world just won't like them, and that's okay.That Vegan lady whose child is on your daughter's soccer team might just teach your daughter0 that healthy eating does not have to mean tasteless (then again, maybe not).

The point is that exposing your children to a variety of people with different personalities, cultures and temperaments will make your children well rounded and complete human beings.On their own, my parents could have never more than pointed me to books on Holland, Africa and the Philippines.They were never fiscally adept enough to save for such luxuries as trips to these exotic locations.Yet their friends exposed me to foods, customs and other experiences that I never would have experienced had it not been for a 'village' mentality.Because of my love for those experiences, I sought more of those types of experiences when it was up to me to expand the village. That led to Chinese, Latino and Native American experiences that could only be described as 'going native.' Thank you, Mom and Dad.

So what is it that stands in your way? I can hear you thinking it: 'I don't have time.' Maybe you can afford to take tours into more countries than I can imagine, but I will tell you what you already know. Tourist experiences are not the same. You can vacation in Acapulco, but it may not rival a home cooked Mexican meal in West Phoenix. You can book a resort in Manila and eat at their five star restaurants, but it won't beat a pit-roasted pig in Sacramento. One of the beauties of our great country is that you do not have to travel the world to give your children awesome experiences. You just have to take the time to get to know the people around you. And while you are at it, you should take the time to really get to know your kids as well.

Chapter 4: Explaining Divorce To Your

Kids

You probably feel a lot like a kid taking home a bad report card, and are dreading telling your children about your divorce. You must remember, children think differently than adults and don't fully grasp the concept of marriage.

Rather than being disappointed in you or judging you for the fact that the marriage has crumbled, they are more likely to be concerned about how divorce will affect them. This should be your focus. Consequently, you need to wait to tell your kids until you are in a relatively stable emotional place. This could mean attending a few therapy sessions or simply taking some deep breaths. Your children need to feel like you're the strong one rather than worry about how they will comfort you.

Breaking the News

When you tell your children you're divorcing, keep it short, simple, and direct. If they know you have been fighting, you can mention this, but don't say, "This probably won't come as a surprise". Divorce is almost always shocking to kids. Here are the cardinal rules of breaking the news:

DON'T use weasel words like probably or maybe. Your children need to know that you are absolutely getting divorced. Don't give them false hope.

DON'T cast blame on your spouse. In fact, if possible, it's best tell your children together.

DON'T tell one child before you tell the other. Otherwise, the child who knows might spill the beans in a way that magnifies the pain of the news. This is the last thing you want.

DON'T get into a discussion about the reason for the divorce. This is an adult issue that you don't need to have your kids deal with.

DON'T judge your child for his reaction. Be prepared for anything — a tantrum, raucous laughter, or maybe even no reaction at all.

DON'T emphasize that a divorce will make you happier or a better person; your child is concerned about their own well-being, not your happiness!

DO emphasize that the divorce is not your children's fault; that you both love them very much, and that their relationships with both parents are going to continue. Children often worry that they won't see the other parent again.

DO wait for a good opportunity to break the news. Hold off until your child is calm, alert, and has time to process the information. For example, it's not a good time to tell them after a bad day at school, or before a birthday, or when your child is totally exhausted.

DO explain to him what divorce means, especially if your child is very young. This is important because it gives you an opportunity to soften the meaning of the word.

DO try using language such as, "Mommy and Daddy have made a hard decision. We think we can be better parents if we live apart".

The Aftermath

After you break the news, don't push your child. Give him a couple of hours to feel his emotions, however they manifest. If he throws a tantrum, don't get angry, and be available to provide emotional support. You must be solely focused on your child, and your soon-to-be-ex, should be too. This is your first opportunity to prove that you can both continue to be loving parents, so don't blow it by getting angry, fighting with your spouse, or focusing on your feelings.

You will also need to be prepared to answer any and all questions. Never refuse to answer a question or criticize your child for her questioning. Instead, answer in an age-appropriate way. If your child asks whose fault the divorce is, for example, explain that both Mom and Dad have realized they just can't get along living together, but will do their best to get along separately.

Be prepared for questions to come in waves. Your child might have very little reaction in the first few hours, but continue to ask questions or feel strong emotions for days or weeks after you first break the news. However, when you or your spouse finally moves out, be prepared for a strong emotional reaction.

Chapter 5: What Is The Reason For

Teaching Children Entrepreneurship?

Why Is It Important?

A constant dilemma: how to raise a child? Parenthood or any other form of children care-taking is one of the most important, if not the most important, part of being an adult. That's why it's good to prepare yourself for that role, or at least constantly upgrade your skills in that area. Well, if you can learn anything, why won't you learn how to raise an extraordinary child?

The role of a parent is extremely complicated. There are no responsibilities or expected results of your methods of upbringing listed, so you can't verify if they're good or not. There are also no regulations, guidelines, or check-off-items - basically, you can do what you want. But fortunately, a human being has instincts. For example, a mother protects her child from danger, even by risking her life, and a father will do anything to pass on his offspring his valuable knowledge and experience.

Despite all of this, we raise our children mainly intuitively, of course with good intentions. But we all know what it's like with good intentions. Sometimes the results of our actions may disappoint us, because good intentions aren't enough without proper knowledge.

But the market never sleeps and comes to rescue! Bookstores offer plenty of guidebooks on how to raise children in a "proper" way, and how to make them behave good and get good grades.

And, almost unanimously, all these guidebooks claim that you can't shout at your children (unless you call it discipline) or punish them (unless it's a part of the consistency in upbringing), and you need to praise them (but be careful at the same time, because it can be demotivating)... In other words, every guidebook claims something different. Which one is to follow, then? How do you know which upbringing method you should choose to raise your child? And how do you know what action should be implemented in a particular situation? Is it better to be consistent or to adjust your reactions to situations? Is it worth teaching children something or let them learn on their own? And everything comes down to a parents' intuitive decision of which "good advice" they'll choose to practice.

Why is entrepreneurship useful?

Since you're reading this, it means that you're more or less aware of the potential of raising entrepreneurial children. Very good!

It's natural that generations pass inexorably. Soon, we're going to give way to our children, and this rule also applies to progress and development, which have accompanied humanity throughout ages. That means one thing: our generation, sooner or later, will pass, and we'll leave our children, who will be in their prime age at any moment, behind. It's them who will contribute to an economic growth and civilization progress. Therefore, our responsibility, as predecessors, is to prepare them for that in the best possible way, and to make them have such traits so that they SURVIVE, and then ADD NEW VALUE to the world.

Since we already know this, we need to ask ourselves several questions: what kind of traits should our children have? What's necessary to survive, and what's inevitable to add value to the world? In other words, what should you teach your children?

What is money for?

Money is predominant in the contemporary world. It's neither good nor bad, it's just the way it is. And if so, the knowledge about money, or, perhaps, what rules it's governed by, is essential.

Firstly, a child will need money to live. Why? Because it's a means of satisfying human needs. And since the money is necessary, one needs to get it somehow. To do so, our children will have two options: either earn it or steal it.

And that's the first choice we need to prepare our soon-to-be-adult children for. We need to do it in such a way that a child knows that stealing is the violation of private property. And since you're not allowed to steal, a child must know HOW to earn money. That's why entrepreneurship is important.

What does it mean to raise "an entrepreneurial child"?

Now it's a good moment to explain how entrepreneurship is understood in this context. Or maybe I'll tell you how I understand entrepreneurship, because I have in mind something different than what the definition of this term tells us. It says: "An entrepreneur is a person who starts and runs a business or organization. An entrepreneur is also called a founder". And I don't want each and every child to establish a company in the future. What I want to persuade you to, dear parents, is strictly associated with the second part of the Wikipedia definition: "He or she develops a business plan, obtains financing and hires employees necessary to run the business. The entrepreneur starts with a good idea for a new business."

In other words, an entrepreneur is a person who comes up with an idea of a company, manages its finances, creates a business plan, and cooperates with employees. To do it properly a person must have particular traits.

That's why in this e-book we'll understand entrepreneurship as a combination of personal traits that make it possible to use all resources available in the most effective way. These traits include: a capability to find or create opportunities, and an ambition combined with the habit of a constant search of how you can do things better than usual. In other words, these are the traits that not only will allow a child to survive, but also function in a society and economy successfully.

As if that wasn't enough, all actions associated with entrepreneurship shape people's characters, what may be useful not only for earning money, but also in everyday situations, where they need to resolve a problem or a conflict, or make a sudden, tough decision.

Moreover, entrepreneurship makes children confident, and parents - proud of them. Why? Because without entrepreneurs the world would stop existing. We need people who are ready to take risks and provide products or services that every average bread eater could buy and use. We need people who are able to see what the needs are, in order to satisfy these needs, without harming either themselves or others.

What am I to do to raise an entrepreneurial child?

What can you give to your child? Oh, very much. Experience. Start-up capital. An ability to independent and creative thinking.

Analyzing the abovementioned examples step by step, experience is what parents want to pass on to their children, but often there are different results. However, there's absolutely nothing wrong with it, but we all know that children often need to experience things in person, so that they learn more effectively.

Not to mention that our experiences may be poor in comparison to what our children are capable of.

As for money, you can give it to your children in different forms. Parents often want to help their children to begin adult life by saving money for buying a car or a flat. And again, there's nothing wrong with that either, but we need to remember that parents aren't obliged to provide their children with material goods. By giving your children money, a car, or a flat, you won't make them either smarter or happier (however, it's obvious that a sixteen-year-old will cry from happiness seeing their own car :)).

Instead, we need to provide them with the ability to cope with life independently.

Finally, it's easier for us, parents, because we live in a time which is favorable. That's because children have an easy access to resources, information, common knowledge, and people.All they need to do is to learn how to find and use all of these.

And while doing so, to form some good habits.
And this is where we play our role, my dear readers.

Chapter 6: Spend Time With Children

There are many opportunities for anyone to get experience taking care of children. Babysitting jobs are almost always available for anyone wanting to get involved and help out parents. Daycare centers are also often hiring, and there are many ways of becoming a professional caretaker. However, even helping out your friends, neighbors, and family members with their children can go a long way into not only getting experience with children, but introducing you to the way parents live their lives.

Spending time with kids one on one is great preparation for your potential life as a parent. During the course of even one night babysitting, you will be playing with the child, preparing and serving him or her meals, getting him or her to get ready for bed, and everything else that forms the basics of day-to-day parental life. Many new parents may not have spent much time with children one on one since their own childhoods, unless they work as elementary school teachers, or in childcare. Even those people could benefit from seeing children in their home environments away from school and day care. One of the advantages of babysitting is that it gives parents the ability to interact with children of various ages, potentially at the same time. If they are babysitting for a family with many children, they may also get some firsthand experience about how to manage sibling rivalry and disagreements.

Babysitters will usually get a preview of common household problems, like kids not wanting to eat certain foods, or not wanting to do homework. It is better to get some experience with these and more serious problems in advance. Your own kids will experience your parenting style far more often than the kids you babysit, for whom you will only be a brief reception to the way they are usually treated. Another advantage of babysitting is giving parents an idea of what parenting is like from the parents' perspective.

As parents, they themselves will have to hire babysitters according to a certain schedule. Prospective parents have the opportunity to interact with current parents, see them in action, and get an idea of what their experiences are like. At the same time, prospective parents will be able to give other people a helping hand in raising their own children. People who may be reluctant to have children or indecisive about it are better off learning that in a relatively consequence-free way as a babysitter, before it is too late.

Chapter 7: Teaching Kids Responsibility

One of the major mistakes that parents make is choosing an elder child to look after the little ones. I remember back in my childhood, this took precedence in my parent's minds. They constantly left the little ones for me to look after and I was expected to give up all of my interests in order to fill their needs and that's not fair. What happens when you do this is that you create an atmosphere between the kids. Kids will argue. They will feel used and the kids that are considered as the underlining will feel that the older child has been given special attention. When children are very small, they should not be left with another child. Choose adults wherever possible.

Creating A Work Schedule

Within the home there are many things that need to be done. As a working parent, you don't have all the time in the world to do everything and kids can earn a little bit of pocket money from effort. If a child likes a particular task, then that's not a bad task to ask that child to do. However, be careful not to have favorites. Instead of saying to the children:

You will do that and your sister will do this

The first question that should be asked of the children is what tasks they actually love doing. If you can get kids to help because they love doing what you ask them to do, then you will get a healthier response. At some time, they also need to understand how important it is to put things away. If a child screws up all of the clothes that you ironed because they couldn't be bothered to put them away, then the child should either wear the clothes in the state they are in or be taught to iron them. I used this trick with an older child and the deal was that anyone who didn't put their clean laundry away would take on the ironing for the week. It soon changed attitudes.

Your partner and you need to be on the same page at all times. For instance, if a child has agreed to do a task and does not do it, then no pocket money is given to the child. You are teaching children that nothing comes for nothing in the world and preparing them to learn all about earning. In fact, you can encourage this further. If you know that a child wants something in particular, put this on your work chart as a goal. Claire wants a new watch that costs $20. Thus, Claire can be encouraged to earn money to gain that watch. Ian wants a new video game. Similarly, he can earn the money to pay half or something like that. Only you know what your finances will allow, but children should be encouraged to do things because you are helping the children learn all about independence and if they learn to do jobs like the following, they will be able to fend for themselves when they are older:

Sewing on buttons
Bringing in the firewood
Cleaning the cutlery drawer
Mending a sock
Cleaning windows
Baking cakes

Learning to clean the car
Tidying their rooms
Putting washing into the wash-bin on time for washday
Helping to fold the clothing
Helping to hang out the clothes to dry
Learning to make beds

These are just a few of the tasks that you can get kids to do. One of my kids actually loved cleaning the toilet and I then found out why. She was placing her brother's toys down the pan and flushing them away! Please know that children have young minds. Thus, keep them away from jobs that are dangerous or that put them into contact with dangerous products.

What Have You Done Today?

One of the most important things that kids need is encouragement and validation. As grown-ups validation isn't as important because grown-ups should have already validated themselves as decent human beings. Kids, however, need that validation until they gain confidence. If you give your kids validation, it makes them feel good and it also helps them to want to do those tasks again. If a kid feels that jobs are torture that parents don't even take any notice of, they see them as punishment. A word of encouragement goes one heck of a long way when you want the kids to help out in the home.

Chapter 8: Connecting On Our Child's

Level

Why Do Kids Throw Tantrums?
Whether your family is enjoying a grand vacation to Disneyland or making a small trip down the street to Walmart, children never fail to make the day epic – both in a good and "not so good" way!
Picture this scenario:
You're out to buy some groceries and brought just enough money to buy whatever is in your shopping list. You weren't able to find a nanny to fill in your mommy duties so you also brought little junior along. Now, junior sees a gigantic chocolate-dipped marshmallow pop and it just so happens to be in the shape of his favorite animal – a rabbit. He looks at you with puppy eyes and says "Mum..." whilst tugging on your shirt and pointing at the candy. You wanted to buy him one but

looking at your wallet and seeing how roomy it is, you realized you simply can't afford another ten bucks added on to your bill. So, you say, "No, we'll have to buy it next time. I don't have enough money today."

Now the conclusion to our little story can (generally) end in two ways: (One) junior is understanding enough to accept the fact that he won't be satisfying his sweet tooth today or (Two) he will start sobbing and even fall seated on the floor, flailing his arms and legs around, and refusing to move any further.

Although the first ending seems like less trouble, chances of it happening are slimmer than Kylie Jenner's waistline. The second one, as you may have guessed, is more likely to happen. And when it does, we usually refer to it as 'temper tantrum'.

But wait, what is a temper tantrum?

Temper tantrums are physical and emotional aggressive reactions a person exhibit when a situation or action displeases him or her. It happens when certain needs and desires are unmet. It is commonly seen in very young children and is characterized by an emotional outburst usually expressed through excessive crying and shouting. Its violent manifestation includes throwing things around and even hitting other people.

Children tend to display these sudden outbursts when they feel external or emotional conflict, as they do not yet know how to express their frustrations the right way. You can think of them as landmines. The moment you step on it, it goes ka-boom! There are several triggers that leads to temper tantrums and some of the root causes are actually much simpler than we think. Below are some of the common triggers I've compiled based on my personal experiences as a mother and the plentiful research I did to address my own kids' episodic tantrums:

Frustration

Children as young as two-years-old do not know what it means to feel frustrated but they do know how it feels. I believe we can all relate to that feeling of disappointment, helplessness, and anger all twisted up together - and boy, does it not feel good!

Even as adults, frustration sometimes gets the better of us. As adults, we tend to be able to exercise more self-control over our emotions. However, most children have yet to develop that life skill. Although throwing a tantrum is definitely not the best way to deal with frustration, I believe it's important to bear in mind that all they're trying to do is to release whatever penned-up negative energy the best way they know how. Let's remember that they've only seen a tenth of our world, so we should always be the bigger person - literally and figuratively-speaking. It does not mean we do nothing to teach them the right way to express their feelings, or to give in every time they throw temper tantrums. However, I've learnt from experience that it is vital as parents to come from a place of understanding as to why kids behave the way they do, and to remain centered so that we can better deal with such situations.

Discomfort

Early childhood is when we begin to interact and form opinions about our environment. Children begin to attribute value to things and people by the roles they play in their lives. They start to create a distinction between "good" things and "not so good" things. They also begin to differentiate between friend and foe — even if their understanding is somewhat distorted.

In essence, taking familiar things away from them and replacing them with new ones can be a very uncomfortable experience for most young children. A very common example can be seen firsthand during a child's first day in kindergarten. Children tend to act out when their parents try to leave them inside an unfamiliar classroom filled with new faces. I've learnt to understand that this is their way of conveying discomfort, and they want to feel safe again. This too, is normal for young children as they are still in the early stages of learning adaptability and independence.

Dissatisfaction

Another common trigger for a temper tantrum is when a child fails to get what he or she wants – as in the case of the scenario you've read earlier. In Freudian Psychology, people are basically driven by the pleasure principle or what they'd call the Id. This pleasure-seeking force is especially strong in newborns and children.

I've learnt that it is essential to examine your child's behavior carefully and see if he or she is driven by any of the factors above; it's always so much easier to effect positive changes to a behavior when we understand its causes.

Why We Should Not Talk To Children Like We Would Our Significant Other

The next question boggling your mind must be about how you can then address your child's tantrum. Well, this part is a bit tricky and figuring it out took a few years off my life! Kidding aside, raising children the right way can be quite challenging – not to mention exhausting.

However, no matter how stressed or tired we may be, let us not forget the power and impact our words have in shaping their personality. They may appear to not be listening, but children are like sponges. They absorb what they hear and observe very well. This is primarily the reason why we must be very careful with our choice of words and how we deliver them.

Specifically, we should avoid talking to our children like we would our significant partners – especially when it comes to matters of character improvement. Unfortunately, despite our good intentions, sometimes our spouses may perceive us as being naggy. We'll do better to relate to our little ones in a different way.

When we interact with our partners, the basic assumption that often holds true is that we are functioning on the same level of reasoning and emotional maturity. When we tell them what we believe is in their best interests, they have the mental and emotional capability to comprehend that. "It's just logical to wash your hands before you eat that ice-cream. That's basic hygiene!" You may tell yourself that, but for young kids, their desire to get a bite off that ice-cream usually overrides whatever 'basic logic' you're telling them.

The reason? They're not at the same developmental stage in life. Also (and again this doesn't ring true for all), when we relay our expectations to our partners, we tend to be perceived by them as being demanding and absolute. Children can't fully comprehend - let alone handle - this kind of pressure and it'll come off as you trying to scold them. This makes them feel unsafe, and guess how they'll usually express that!

The early stages of life are crucial to character building and our words and actions are all very important factors that can greatly influence how our kids turn out. Let's take a short break to ponder over some questions:

Who are you as a parent? What is your main role in raising your kids?

What is your parenting style? Do you let your kids learn things the hard way through experience or do you prefer to teach them so they can avoid making mistakes in the first place?

Do you truly understand your child? What makes your child tick? Does your child respond better to carrots or to sticks?

How effective is your communication with your child? Do you gain a deeper understanding of your child after each interaction or do you go, "boy, it's really hard to figure you out!"

Throughout the next chapters, keep in mind your honest answers and ensure your actions align with your beliefs.

Understanding Our Child's Way Of Thinking

The communication barriers between parent and child usually lies in the differences in their cognitive thinking. There are simply so many things adults like us are capable of comprehending that are still foreign to the minds of young kids.

According to Jean Piaget, a Swiss psychologist and epistemologist renowned for his pioneering work in child development, people undergo four different stages of cognitive development that begin the moment they are born up to the time they retire. Toddlers or young children usually fall on the 2nd stage of cognitive development – the preoperational stage (1).

At the preoperational stage, all that most children know is the world of "Me" and "I". To them, the world revolves around them and everything needs to go their way. Anything otherwise often leads to tantrums. They're not deliberately being stubborn; they are simply at a stage in their lives whereby they find it difficult to view things from another person's perspective. Knowing this allows us as parents to comprehend things from our kids' perspective, and to craft our response to their behavior accordingly.

Chapter 9: Top Common Single Parent

Fears

Having been a single parent herself, this writer knows the awesome fear of worrying about her children while she is at work, and the even greater fear that the child might be snatched by her foreign ex-husband.

Whether you were married to a foreigner or not, the same fears apply - and a man too who is a single father might fear that his children might be kidnapped. One of the worst fears in a nutshell is that one day she will get a call from the child's school or the father to say that something has happened to the child.

Single parents, especially mothers, are less concerned about things like food and clothes as those are situations which can be easily remedied. She is worried constantly about the welfare of the child.

Most Dreaded Five Common Single Parent Fears

The number one fear a parent has after a messy and complicated divorce is that her partner has more money than she has and will get custody of the children as he has the financial means to do more for the children and draw things out. He has money to hire a detective or the best lawyer money can buy and that the judge might think she is not on equal footing and that he might get the children. Another dreaded fear that a single parent has is that while he or she is at work that the other parent will come to the school, take the child, and run off with the child to his country.

Even though there are laws against this, once a single parent snatches a child and runs off to a foreign country, there is a lot of work involved as it involves international law and there is a lot more than the kidnapping charge to deal with, all of which will drag out the process.

The single parent will fear that the other parent although he or she loves the child, will not put the interests of the child first and will stop at nothing to have the child in his or her possession as at that time neither parent can think clearly, and she fears that she might never see the child again.

A child kidnapping has the same devastating psychological effects on a parent as a child that is missing or found dead. Another common single parent fear is that something will happen to her like an accident or a long illness and that her children will be taken away by the authorities and that she will not be able to look after her children herself.

While it might seem to be an irrational fear, there are single parents who even though their children are asleep at night, worry that someone might break into the house at night, and so she sleeps with a baseball bat next to the bed or a knife under the pillow.

Single mothers are fierce children protectors. A parent also fears that when he or she sends the children for the weekend or holidays to the other parent's house, that the children might not be returned.

Chapter 10: The Consistent Parent

We all appreciate consistency in our lives, but it's even more important when raising children. They learn from routine and are, in fact, comforted by it. This is the premise behind the educational system. A routine or "norm" is established and the learning is introduced in expected levels and frequencies.

Put yourself in a child's world for a moment. Let's say it is a school day and you are in the third grade.

A consistent day might include:

rising and breakfast at home at a certain time

catching the bus at the regular stop and arriving at school at about the same time

reporting to the same teacher's room and taking your normal seat

eating a hot lunch in the cafeteria at the same time

boarding the bus at the normal time and being dropped off at home

An inconsistent version of that day might include:

getting up at whatever time and eating whatever is in the refrigerator

missing the bus so walking to school in the rain, tardy and in trouble

wandering into any teacher's room and sitting on the floor because the seats are all filled

no lunch because there was no money or lunch bag prepared

boarding the wrong bus and having to walk two miles home only to discover the front door locked and no neighbors at home

While this may seem an extreme example, it's not so difficult to imagine that one or two of these scenarios could happen quite easily in a disorganized household. The most startling realization, though, is that the only difference between the two scenarios is consistency. It is so simple to have a well-ordered life.

There is no question that life is filled with unexpected events. That makes establishing a "norm" all the more important for children. One of the most important "norms" to establish has to do with discipline.

Discipline is based upon a given set of rules and consequences for lack of compliance. As adults, we are presented with laws, conducts of behavior, regulations, permits, employee manuals, taxes and more. Everything is spelled out clearly and that means that everyone is agreement as to what sort of behavior is, or is not, allowed. The penalties for breaking these regulations are equally publicized. Thus, if you don't observe the rules, you know what punishment is in store for you.

Children need the same sort of rules and penalty definition. This not only gives parents guidelines, but prepares the children for following rules throughout their lives.

Rules need to be age appropriate but consistent. When your 16-year-old daughter is not permitted on car dates, the same rule needs to apply four years later with your next daughter. The same needs to be in place for boys—and this should not depend on whether any of the children are particularly responsible, or not. That builds animosity between children and leaves so much gray area that you will have difficulty enforcing even the most gentle rules if you can't stick with the tough ones.

Be consistent and you'll find your job far easier.

Chapter 11: Your Child And Your Love Life

Your partner or partners: when one is young and energetic having the entire world eating at the palm of his hand, commanding all to dance for his music; it comes as no surprise that when maturity kicks in on such an impulsive fellow, reality hits hard and the chickens come home to roost. Because we are all prone to choosing incompatible partners, if no other reason exist for us to be thorough in making this choice, this very ineptitude in choosing compatible partners ought to be the very one that dictates thoroughness in our choices. Choosing a potential lover ought not be limited to things like trimmed abdomen with the popular six or four 'packs', the curves and the biceps as though we are recruiting Mr. or Miss Universe.

Displaying your affection: once you have made your choice on who should share your laughter, sadness, joys and worries, successes and failures. Now is the time to hold hands, kiss, stare at each other for no reason at times, prolong the hugs and continuously reassuring each other about your undying love, doing all this in your private space. When you do all of this, you ought not to have other people in mind but your partner. As soon as your child takes up space in your mind while you are having a private moment with your partner to an extent that thinking about the child interferes with that wonderful moment, it is possible that you have a very weak bond and poor relationship with your child. In my opinion a child whose biological parents are no longer in each other's lives should have been assured by the parent she or he lives with that, the presence or the absence of a 'new mother/father' in your life can never replace and diminish your love for your child.

This promise to the child ought to be carefully backed up with consistent reassurance in deeds such as giving the child the due attention each time s/he needs it. Deliberately display your affection in the presence of the child so the child can familiarize him/herself with the parent's happiness and love life. This is positive reinforcement for the child's view of what a loving relationship ought to be like between two loving parents.

The connection between you and your child is stronger than you think. This is more evident in cases where children presents a repulsive behaviour when that connection is threatened by the new arrival in your life. Once the child figures out that there are missing activities in both your lives and the new arrival is likely to be the cause, your child would most likely act it out in the best way they only know how. Some children would go out of their way seeking means and ways to punish you for this undesirable change by pulling all sorts of stunts. Most common of these stunts are the out of control behaviour and trouble making seeking your attention. It is very important for the parents to reassure children that they care about anything which might be of importance to the child at all times. During your very busy schedule, just take a moment and LISTEN to what your child have to say rather than dismissing him or her in protest "I told you I'm very busy"; it could be that it is a matter of life and death or even if it is not that, the child could be 'dying' to tell you something that would determine both your relationship from that moment forth.

Children often resents their parent's partner(s) based on how often the partners get to have all the attention from you in comparison to them (children).

But when it comes to how frequent you change your partners, displaying your affection might be a hard thing to do because of a number of reasons. When you share the same space and love with your child and your lover or partner, remember that your child and your partner would inevitably form their own special bond, particularly so if they do not have overwhelming repulsive issues between them. Children, because of their immature emotional intelligence, often resist change in general but in particular seem to be vehemently opposed to fickle behavioural patterns of their parents more so in regards to the frequent introduction of 'new daddies/mums'.

What makes children uncomfortable when parents display affection: when a child has never been exposed to parental affection at a very young age, this could be a difficult concept to grasp at a later date. Further complications are often caused by parents who would constantly present irreconcilable behavioural patterns such as aggressive behaviour in general around the house and once in a while, when your mood is in cloud nine, you then present a fit-of-love shocking the children's fragile emotional intelligence. When the primary parent (by primary parent I refer to the biological parent of the child) suffers abuse in the presence of the child, the child tends to lose trust for any new parent who would be introduced in their life in the fear that history could repeat itself. In such cases permanent mistrust could develop into a complex incurable disease of the soul.

A story is told of a widower who took a wife out of concern for his five year old son. The man returned from his out of country business trip one night and asked his son how was his relationship with the new mum. To his surprise the boy started off by saying "My new mum does not lie to me like my old mum. My old mum used to lie to me. When I would play with my friends till late she would say that I am not going to get food but then she would give me some before I go to bed. But the new mum, when she says that I'm not going to get food, she means it, it is three days now since I ate anything."

Chapter 12: Here Is How It Works:

Your child throws a fit while you are desperately trying to shop. She is physically and verbally escalated and creating a huge uproar. After separating yourself and the child from the stimulus (toys, cereal, candy, etc.) you determine that the best course of action is a Time Out – to allow the child time to calm down. Finding a quiet and private place, you instruct your child that when she is calm you will begin the time. (Remember: Time Out is not used for anything other than the establishment of emotional and mental control. It is NOT the discipline moment. Before we continue, I want to caution that it is possible for the child to calm down and regain control as you head to a location to do a Time Out. If this is the case then you would move to the teaching phase immediately.)

You determine that your five-year-old is developmentally five and so that is the number of minutes you will use.You remain near the child and take your own time to calm and collect your emotions and thoughts.As the child's body uses up the energy it created in the fight, she will be able to sit more and more still. Do not get caught up in the insistence that she remain still; remember that, due to the processes of the primitive brain, she is most likely **unable** to.Battling for extreme physical compliance will only destroy your joy in parenting.Letting her fidget and wiggle will actually hasten the process and help her calm. Once the child is in a state of refraction, you will know it by observing her physical state. Typically, a body in emotional refraction will have little energy and may even appear limp. Verbal conversation can be very drawn and labored.It is in this very open state that you have your best opportunity for teaching and discussion.If you are not present and miss this moment, the child will have entered into a state of homeostasis and she will be closed to the learning that could have been. This only frustrates the child and destroys the bliss you are seeking from the Time Out. This is often the case when a child is sent to their room for Time Out. Unless you are there to observe the child and see her enter into the teaching moment of emotional refraction, you will have missed the opportunity for teaching, for discipline, and can expect many more escalations like the one you just endured. When you act in the teaching moment, ask the child why she feels you gave her the Time Out. Use the word "feel" as it is more powerful than the word "think" in engaging the limbic brain that was active when the Time out was being implemented. Ask her what she was feeling prior to the outburst. Validate her emotion and the desire to tantrum when she felt unheard, even if you feel it is silly or irrelevant. Many times this is all she wants—to be heard and validated. When it gets right down to it, isn't this all any of us wants? Discuss with the child what she can do in the future when she feels like this again. The space of time in which the window of refraction is open can be different with every event. Timing the teaching well will allow you to reach the child. Do not over do it. Ask questions and reflect. Let the child find much of the learning on her own, with your guidance.

If you feel that there is a logical and natural consequence directly related to the outburst, now is a good time to discuss and impose it. CAUTION!! Do not impose a consequence solely based on the behavior leading to the Time Out. If teaching has taken place and you were able to correct the behavior no additional consequence is needed. To impose it would be punishing. Additionally, the discussion during the refraction period is a perfect time to establish the when/then rules for next time. For example, "When you have an emotional outburst in (situation), then a Time Out will be necessary," coupled with the positive consequence for good behavior, "When you (appropriate behavior) then you will earn (reward)". This is also be the time that together you establish the appropriate consequence for any future failures to maintain the rule/appropriate behavior.

An optional route to Time Out that we employed quite often when our kids were young was Time out (for the toy).Often a simple solution to an argument over a toy (or anything) is to simply remove it by placing it in Time Out.This is not to imply to the children that the toy was behaving rather than the kids. Rather, it is a way to initiate non-blaming, problem-solution oriented dialogue.Removing the toy in this manner gives a chance to instruct the children on proper play and conflict resolution, without the danger of shame and blame to the kids. They are taught teamwork and cooperation as they learn to play together while sharing the same toy.You teach them children that they can share and when they share the toy does not have to have a Time Out for creating problems. You can use this as an opportunity to talk with them about managing emotions and communicating needs/wants. Once the children have calmed down, the toy is brought out of

Time Out and they are given a chance to try the new collaborative skills. It is important that you remain there with them during this exploration of new skills to help guide them through the process.

As bold as it may sound, nearly all events leading to a Time Out can be avoided when you are actively engaged in the child's behavior and utilize **all** the tools available.Even more important, however, is the asking yourself the question "Why do I care?" to assess what is happening within your own emotional arousal.Powerful tools such as establishing situational rules, pre-determining consequences, understanding the need driving the behavior, and many others are explored in detail in my book **Discipline for a Change**.Although it is not possible to be there with the child at all times, when true discipline is used to effectively teach children to govern themselves, the hard job of parenting is much, much easier. When Time Out is reserved **only** for those intervening when all other methods have been ineffective, the child will respect it as a sign that something needs to change. Effective dialoging afterward, before the child returns to their "normal" state, further decreases the likelihood of them repeating this same behavior.

I want to close with a story. While shopping a few days ago, I watched a father trying to calm his screaming daughter while her mother was in a dressing room. I tensed, waiting for the worst, because most times I have observed similar interactions in which the child ends up getting punished because they will not "STOP IT AND CALM DOWN!" In those cases, things usually go from bad to worse because the parent is embarrassed by the looks from others. But in this case—to my great relief—the father tirelessly worked to comfort, hold, talk to, and rock his upset daughter. Finally, the mother came out and they were able to leave. This impressive, implacable, and patient man was an amazing example of the true joy, freedom, and connection that can exist even in trying times, through the power of positive principled parenting.

Imagine the immediate and long-term impact on your children, your communities, and our entire nation if parents everywhere learned how to respond in such a way to upset or misbehaving children!

One family, one parent, one child at a time, we can get there! I wish you well as you raise your children and encourage you to continue to seek out tips and tools to decrease the stress of being a parent.

Chapter 12: Toddler Proofing Your House

Toddler proofing your house refers to creating a safe environment for your toddler. Although it might seem like your house is a safe place, there can be a million dangerous things lying around.

Here is looking at a room-by-room toddler-proofing guide to follow.

Kitchen

The first room to toddler proof will be the kitchen. There will be many dangers present in there necessitating attention.

The first step will be to remove the detergents, cleaning equipment, bleach and other such supplies from the lower shelves/cabinets. Children can get extremely curious and reach for these. They might also be tempted to open the bottles. It will, therefore, be best to either move these to a higher place or lock the cabinets that contain these.

Next, make sure that pots, pans, and other heavy utensils are not hanging down or within your child's reach. They might get curious and decide to play with them. The same extends to forks and knives. Ensure that they are safely stowed away in higher places out of reach for your child. Remember that they will soon be able to open drawers and so it will not be safe to store them there. You can also install childproof drawer locks if necessary.

It will be extremely important to keep prescription medication, tablets, and multivitamins away on higher shelves. Children might think of it as candy and reach for them.

Keep toasters, kettles and other such appliances out of their reach. The wires should be coiled and tucked away with the appliances. Push them as far back on the ledge as possible so that there is no danger of the item tumbling over.

Small items such as magnets, trinkets and other things on the fridge door and inside it should be stored away.

Attach safety covers to stove knobs so that your toddler is unable to turn them.

Buy kitchen rugs that do not skid. The ones with rubber bottoms that stick to the floor will make for good options.

Living room

Toddlers will be extremely social and spend most of their time in the living room. It will, therefore, be quite important to safeguard it. Here is looking at the different measures to adopt for this area of the home.

It will be extremely important to add corner protectors to furniture corners and padding to sides of tables, you must add cushioning so that your toddler does not get hurt.

If your furniture is placed close to windows, then move it away so that your baby does not get near the window. It will especially be important if these are easy for your child to climb up on. Alternatively, use locks that do not allow the window to be opened by a child.

If you have expensive pieces of decor in the room such as vases, paintings, and other such items, then keep them stored away. Toddlers will not understand that these are expensive and end up knocking them over while playing.

Remember that curtain cords and blind cords that hang low can prove to be choking hazards. It will be important to place these as high as possible so that they are not available to your child.

Children love to play with remote controls and might end up harming their eyes.

Cover the television cabinet or lock up the television so that your child is unable to reach it. It is also advised to secure television cabinets, wall units, shelves to the wall, as your child may use these at some point to hold onto, and the excess pressure may make the item to be vulnerable to tipping over, hurting your toddler.

If you have pets at home then they should be slowly introduced to your baby. All pets love children and will be welcoming of a new play partner. Allow the pet to sniff the baby and get used to having him around. This will make for an easier transition as baby becomes a toddler for both pet and child to stay safe.

Toddler's room

The next room to toddler proof will be the toddler's room. If you have a nursery already set up then there are minimal changes you will need to make, however, if you are setting you your nursery here are the steps to follow.

The first step will be to deal with the crib. The crib has to be as safe and secure as possible as your baby/toddler will spend quite some time in it. Ensure that it is made of good quality wood that meets current safety approval guidelines. It will be best not to use metal as the surface can irritate your child's skin and he/she might get hurt while standing up.

It will be best to place a large, soft rug close to the crib so that it can catch your toddler if in case they decide to climb out from the crib. The rug will also make for a great option for your toddler to crawl when they grow older.

Stow away all the toys and other baby goods in boxes and bins. They can pose danger to your children who can tumble over them. Make sure these boxes are within your child's reach, as otherwise, they will try to climb up to reach them, which can prove to be dangerous.

Move away small objects from the crib and the room, especially if your baby is less than 6 months old. In fact, it will be important to move away pillows and blankets as well as they too can pose danger for your baby. Keep them stored away until it is safe to pull out for your child.

Lamps and bulbs should be as high up as possible. They can get quite hot and hurt your baby.

Place finger pinch guards in between door hinges so that they do not pinch your baby's fingers. The same extends to the hinges on the crib that have foldable gates.

Bathroom

The bathroom needs special attention, as it can be a little slippery. You will have to put in measures to safeguard it for your toddler so that he or she does not get hurt.

Keep all the soaps and other toiletries high up so that your toddler is unable to reach them. The same extends to cleaners and other such liquids.

Try to keep the toilet closed as much as possible. Young toddlers that are not potty trained can get curious. Place something on top of the lid so that they do not lift it up. Keep all electric appliances away from the bathtub and sink. They can pose danger for your child.

If you have medicines in the bathroom, then keep them locked away so that your child cannot access them.

Remove mats that are slippery so that they do not slip over them.

Make sure you keep an eye on them at all times, especially if they run into the bathroom. They might try to lock themselves in, so ensure the locks and latches are out of their reach.

Garden

It will also be important to toddler proof the garden. Remove broken pots that can potentially harm your child.

It will be best to cordon off the garden so that your toddler cannot access areas where you do not want them to be.

Remember, it will be best to toddler proof the house well in advance. Don't leave it to the last minute and try to prepare for your baby to become a mobile toddler several months in advance.

Here is some safety equipment to consider buying and installing in your home.

CCTV Cameras

You can buy and install cameras in the house so that you can keep an eye on your child. This is especially important if you have an adventurous and active child at home. Place the cameras in all the rooms and connect the system to your phone so that you can keep an eye on your child's activities. This is also useful if you go to work leaving your child back at home in the care of someone else.

Gates, fences

Gates and fences will come in handy when you wish to safeguard your toddler. They can be placed in different places such as the garden and staircases so that your toddler remains safe and free from danger. Buy good quality gates and fences that are guaranteed to safeguard your child.

Walkie talkies

Walkie-talkies can be used to speak to your child if he or she is in another room. This will bridge communication and encourage the child to talk more. If you leave your child at home with a caregiver, consider calling the child to get the child to update you on what the child is up to. It will be a fun way to keep an eye on the toddler and teach them to communicate.

Chapter 13: The Five Types Of Ex-Spouse

Relationships

Let's take a look at the five different kinds of ex-spouse relationships that you will commonly seen after divorce.If you've already gone through a divorce, try to see yourself in these five different types.If you're currently going through divorce or thinking about it, focus on the one that will help your child be emotionally secure for the rest of their life. Whether you want to believe it or not, you have the ability to make a CHOICE about what kind of relationship you will have with your ex-spouse. They may not agree, but you can hold to your promise to react I only positive ways for the sake of your child.

Cooperative Colleagues: This type of couple is able to cope with their anger in productive, positive ways.They manage their conflicts well and do not allow their kids to be caught in the middle of a dysfunctional or angry situation. This group of divorced people is able to separate their unhappiness with their spouse from their parental responsibilities. This takes a high level of maturity on the part of both people, but it is in the best interests of the child. For instance, even if one parent has made the other angry about something, they do not allow the child to hear them talk about it or see them upset.

Perfect Pals: The second group of couples is also amicable. They are in a very small, but important, minority of couples who remain best friends after the divorce. They may still do things together, but maintain a nonsexual relationship. Sometimes, these relationships will have conflicts where anger flares up at times, but they remain in a close and caring relationship. This can be a great situation for kids as long as the children understand that this does not mean their parents are getting back together. The risk of sending mixed signals can be high, so it's important to communicate with the child effectively.

Angry Associates: Unfortunately, the remaining 50% of couples usually fall into the typical stereotypes that we hear about divorce. These couples are often archenemies. The Angry Associates are often known by the anger they display at each other. The way they express their anger is not normally just confined to the differences they had in marriage. It actually works its way into every relationship in the family. This overriding anger greatly affects the kids who have likely had to witness it during the marriage and after it was over.

Fiery Foes: This group is what we typically see when we think of the bad divorce. The couple has rage for one another which filters into their family lives and causes distress and pain for years after the divorce. These are the ones that end up in custody battles for years or may even wind up in the news media. Often, revenge fuels violence and anger for years and years.

Dissolved Duos: This group comprises ex-spouses who have no contact with one another. In fact, one parent will often disappear completely from his or her child's life.Thankfully, this is a rarity even after contentious divorces.

Ages and Stages of Child Development

All children go through specific stages of development as they grow from being infants to young adults.Each of these stages has its own components and challenges as the brain is developing.Although the following information are really just approximations, most people do go through these developmental stages because they are genetically determined.

It's important to understand that some children may be behind or ahead of the stages simply because every person's human development is unique.In addition, our environment can play a critical role in how advanced or behind we are at any given time in the developmental outline.

Each stage of growth is made up of several factors including intellectual development, physical development, emotional development and language and social development.Hopefully, parents going through a divorce will be able to focus on the fact that their children are still growing up and going through the stages of development.Otherwise, a child can get stunted emotionally by the turmoil surrounding a bitter divorce.

Understanding these important milestones is critical for making sure that the damage from a divorce is minimal to a child.

The Stages of Development

Infants and Babies: 0 to 2 years old

In this time of development, is very important for parents to understand the challenges of raising another human being.The bonds developed during this time will last a lifetime.Parents can contribute to this stage of development by learning to understand, encourage and respect this new human being.During this time, parents learn who their child really is.

Obviously, if a divorce happens early on in a child's life at this stage of development, one parent may miss out on some important milestones and bonding with the child.Kids at this age won't have many obvious memories, but the bonding that takes place is critical for both parent and child.

Toddlers and Preschoolers: 2 to 5 years old
Here children start to get older and take their first steps as this new phase of development commences.Kids are now able to roam around freely in their own world and explore their environment.This is where the development of language puts them into the world around them.

Learning the names of objects and gaining the ability to ask for what they want, kids will uncover their independent side during this stage.Parents often refer to part of the toddler development stage as being the "terrible twos" because kids learn to say no.

One of the big challenges during this stage of development is teaching children how to regulate their emotions.Temper tantrums and meltdowns are pretty common during this period, but the bonding during the toddler and preschool years can help to teach kids how to express themselves emotionally in a proper way.

If a child is going through a contentious divorce during this age, it can be very upsetting emotionally. Because they are already on the edge with emotional expression, having parents around them who are arguing and fighting can only add negativity to the situation. After all, if the child witnesses their parents not being able to regulate their own emotions, it stands to reason that they will not succeed during this stage of development.

During this stage, toddlers also need to learn to accept the word NO from others. If a parent is going through a divorce and feels guilty about it, they might be tempted to always say yes to everything. This doesn't allow the child to learn the important reality that some people are going to tell them no. Because of this, they react quite emotionally when someone tells them no if those parents are suffering from guilt and letting them get away with everything.

During the toddler and preschooler stage of development, intellect is also greatly improved.This is in preparation for kids to begin school and start learning how to interact with their peers.Kids also get stronger physically during this time, and they start learning how to master new skills.Parents can be an encouragement and positive force during this time.

School Age Children: 6 to 12 years old

Raising kids at school age can be a great experience as parents watch them try new activities, become their biggest cheerleader during their accomplishments and watch them achieve success with their grades and academics.

However, in some circumstances there is a lot of frustration during this stage of development.Kids have to learn how to accept themselves and be independent in the face of being around all different kinds of children.Parents also have to learn how to accept their own strengths and weaknesses as they navigate the tricky waters of raising the child or children.

If you're going through a divorce during this stage, it can be quite difficult for ex spouses to co-parent the child.After all, having both parents show up at an athletic event when they are in the middle of a custody battle or are just consistently angry with each other can be extremely detrimental to the child.Plus, discipline and other important parental obligations and decisions must be made by both parents.If not, one parent feels slighted and the other one feels like they have to carry a heavy load.

In the middle is the child who is afraid to upset the apple cart.They're trying to learn who they are and enjoy the school-age years while their parents are still dragging them back and forth through a divorce that may have happened a while ago. This can leadproblems in school or discipline issues as a child tries to "fight back" by being combative with their parents.

School-age kids do not need the constant supervision that younger ones do.They're starting to assert more independence which can be a problem after a divorce. One parent may not be the disciplinarian that the other one is which can cause fights about allowing the child to be too independent or not independent enough.

If the parents are consistently fighting with each other, the child may never learn how to make good choices or develop their own self-discipline because they don't have good role models to watch. This is also the time that a moral code is instilled in the child. If you have one parent who has a different moral compass than the other, this can lead to a confusing situation for the child.

Giving praise and encouragement during the school-age years is very important and must come from both parents in order to provide emotional stability going forward. This requires that parents work together rather than being combative with each other at the exclusion of the child's feelings.

Adolescence and Teenagers: 13 to 18 years old

Adolescence can be one of the trickiest parts of the parenting journey.Kids are well within the developmental stage where they want to assert their independence, yet they also do not always make the best decisions.

During the teen years, kids will often try to act out, especially if they are looking for attention.They are caught between being a kid and being an adult, and their brain often doesn't work quickly enough to make the right kinds of decisions.

Middle school can be a difficult time because a child's body is changing from that of a kid to an adult.Bullying has also become a major issue in many schools, so parents must work together to be on the lookout for any signs of their child is being bullied or has become the bully at their school.

Middle schoolers often have passive aggressive behavior, self-doubt and self consciousness. They often need to be encouraged and complimented about how they look and how they are doing in school. They might doubt their value as a person and their future.In some cases, they may be overly confident and experience moodiness on a regular basis. Remember that hormones are raging during this time.

Then you have high school where kids start to define who they are and what they want for their future.They develop skills to move forward to get good jobs or go to college.Their talents start to get perfected and their social skills are important.Peer pressure is at an all-time high and relationships become very important.

There is a lot of temptation involved in high school.Drugs, alcohol and sex are the primary temptations that many kids are exposed to during these years. If they don't feel loved or supported at home, they become prime targets for these sorts of issues. During this time of middle school and high school, adolescents need their parents more than ever which can become a real issue in a divorce situation.If the parents aren't on the same page or aren't even communicating all, kids can easily fall through the cracks and make some very bad, life-changing decisions during this time of life.

The way that a child deals with a divorce can vary quite a bit depending upon a number of factors including the age the child is at the time of the separation and subsequent divorce. Of course, there are other things that matter during this process as well including:
• The amount of conflict between the parents
• Communication and openness in being able to discuss the divorce with both parents
• Any added stress including changing schools, moving to a new home or one parent getting remarried
• How the home life was for the child before the divorce
• How involved the nonresidential parent is after the divorce
• Any economic problems going on within the family
• The parenting skills of both parents

- How the residential parent adjusts to being divorced
- Love and approval from both parents

As you can see, there are many different factors that can cause a child to have difficulties after a divorce no matter what stage of development they are at.

Children can get stressed out just like adults do. Unfortunately, adults know that they can go speak with a counselor or talk to a friend about their problems, while many children don't want to discuss these things with their parents. They might be embarrassed, afraid or not want to burden their parents with anything else. They see the torment and upset that the divorce caused their parents, and they certainly don't want to add to that by speaking about their feelings.

Chapter 14: Essential Lessons On

Emotional Skills

So far, we have covered various aspects of encouraging learning in your child. In some cases, this may be all you need to know. However, it is equally important that your kid learn how to deal with emotions from early childhood as well. The reason for this is quite subjective. While children have different ways of dealing with emotions, learning how to vent them may go a long way in ensuring that they are happy in the end. Moreover, when your child learns to deal with emotions, it can prevent some of the complications that come with negative emotions such as low self-esteem, depression and reduced interest in learning. In fact, your child is more likely to be receptive to learning when they are happy and content than when they are struggling emotionally. You can ensure that your child learns how to deal with emotions, both positive and negative, and nurture love at a young age through different methods, depending on your child.

Emotional development starts straight from birth, when your child learns how to trust and enjoy your company, and of those who care for them. During the early days of your child's life, he/she is able to read and interpret facial expressions and can tell when you have negative or positive emotions by simply looking at your face keenly. It is at this time that you should teach them empathy, as they are bond to learn from cues of love from those around him/her. While in some instances you may not have control over your child's emotional development, especially when you are not with them, you can still do a couple of things at home. For starters, make sure that you spend a lot of time with your child, especially during the first years of their development. In addition, be sure to portray positive emotional cues like smiling often.

While your child may seem small at a glance, their brain consists of about 1000 billion cells (close to the stars in the Milky Way), which are selectively sieved during childhood. This means that your child is able to absorb plenty of information, as this is the time the child's brain is most flexible. Create a positive living environment for your child, both emotionally and socially. Practice reading books to your child, even if he/she is merely a year old or less and cannot understand what you are reading to them. With time when they start speaking, make a point of letting them read to you too, although most of the time they will just be making sounds and pointing at images.

Reading to your child from early age has been proven to help in brain development. Moreover, when you notice that your child is sick or upset, comfort them regularly. On the other hand, teach your kid to respect other people's property while they are still young. For instance, while playing baseball, you could encourage him to play outside in order not to break something.

Learn to study your child's emotional cues, and praise them when they have done something good, even if not successful, just for the effort. It is also a great idea to let your child have their way sometimes. For instance, you could let them choose their favorite color of socks or shirt once in a while. This will go a long way in boosting their self-confidence.

Chapter 15: Positive Discipline

Positive discipline is an alternative way of disciplining children. It is based on the works of Alfred Adler and Rudolf Dreikurs. This is a method by which the focus is on the positive side of a behavior. The prevailing idea is that children are all essentially good; they only behave in a good or bad way. Good behaviors are taught and reinforced while bad behaviors are weaned without the need for physical and verbal cruelty. This is very different from simply ignoring negative behaviors. Parents are rather encouraged to actively participate in teaching and helping the child learn how to behave appropriately while maintaining a calm, respectful, and loving manner towards the child.

Positive discipline utilizes all the reinforcement and punishment types. It makes use of positive reinforcement (e.g., praise for good behavior), negative reinforcement (e.g., ignoring whining), positive punishment (e.g., have the child put back thrown toys), and negative punishment (e.g., withholding desirable privileges for negative behavior). There are a lot of ways to train a child, without having to resort to violence, yelling, and scolding. It can be done in a loving and caring manner. Most parents will think that children will not listen if they do not yell or talk loudly to their child. Researches show that children are more likely to listen and obey when treated respectfully and lovingly than when treated harshly.

The golden rule in positive discipline is that parents treat their children in a way that they want their children to treat them. It is based on the kind of relationship that parents have with their children. Secure and trusting parent-child relationship is a good foundation for positive discipline. The ultimate goal of discipline should be teach and allow children to develop self-control and self-discipline, not to have complete control over the child's behavior.

There are five criteria in positive discipline. These are:

1. Belonging and significance

Positive discipline primarily aids the child to feel that he or she is loved. It does not alienate the child and making him feel unwanted because of a misdeed.

2. Kindness and Firmness

Teaching and correcting is done while maintaining respect, both for the parents and the child. Correcting behaviors is done kindly and lovingly but in a firm manner.

3. Consideration of the child's feelings

The child is also a person. Discipline takes into account the child's feelings, and opinions. The child is allowed to think for himself, plan for his future and is given some allowance to decide on what changes to make in his behavior. This approach has a more long-term effect on the child.

4. Teaching life and social skills

Discipline is not only limited to teaching good behaviors. Rather, positive discipline allows the child to learn the impact of his actions not only on the self but also to others. It teaches children to respect and have concern for the self as well as for others.

5. Encourages responsibility

Children are allowed to learn what they are capable of doing. They are also taught how to use these abilities constructively. Responsible use of personal power and capabilities is taught and reinforced.

Chapter 16

Over the last thirty five years or so, there have been a number of countries that have outlawed the physical reprimand of children. Gradually, over time, about one country each year has been added to the list, banning corporal punishment of children in the home. You might investigate this for yourself and discover well over one hundred countries prohibit corporal punishment in schools. Yet it remains legal for a parent to spank their child in the United States. In all of North America, physical punishment by a parent, as long as it is not severe, is still seen by many as a necessary discipline, and condoned, orencouraged.

There's difficulty in changing the cultural attitude that corporal punishment is an effective means of discipline. Many view prohibiting spanking as limiting the rights of parents. The underlying assumption, unfortunately, is that children remain the property of adults and subtly serve their parents' self-esteem issues. That's not fair to say though, because legally, a parent's lack of child rearing that results in an unruly youngster playing havoc and destroying property can be held legally liable. Perhaps their defense would be that the law didn't allow corporal punishment.

No matter, times change things. Before the civil rights movements of the sixties, spanking happened in almost every household in the United States. The practice has declined since. Despite efforts from social behavior authorities, it hasn't changed as much as you might think. Parents still use physical punishment today. They carry the traditions of home life they themselves were conditioned to. Yet, because of social pressures, they openly or emotionally express remorse for their actions along with their scant conviction that it advances their child's conduct.

How to control one's angry impulses is one of the things you try to teach your children. Spanking, when done in an angry way, sabotages this teaching. Any available spanking commentary will usually give warnings, based on scientific research, to never spank in anger. Experts claim if this were truly practiced, almost all corporal child punishment wouldn't occur, because once the parent calms down, he or she would come up with a more appropriate method of correction.

Recent studies show some startlingly facts. You may even be surprised when searching web-sites. In the United States, more than nine out of ten 3- and 4-year-olds have been spanked. A majority of parents condone this tradition and use it as a regular form of behavior modification. Despite all the psychological damage that the so-called experts claim, face it. Spanking a toddler has been a long-time custom. Currently, parents who administer bodily reprimands were often on the receiving end themselves. In other words, the cause of this form of "educational" forcefulness are often hidden in the repressed history of the parents. Consequently, adults pay little attention or possibly do not understand the connections between their previous experiences involving some form of psychological grievance and those they actively repeat in the present. So, not at all in a personal begrudging way, they perpetuate a slightly disparaging cycle by inflicting similar suffering on their offspring.

Let's get back to the happy home life syndrome with a excitedly fulfilled marital state. Imagine your toddler or children being angry and disobedient in this type of environment. That probably would make no sense. But if there is, it would most likely be minor compared to an unfulfilled, cheerless, and stale upbringing.

Putting marital failures aside, the next generation continues to carry the damage that has been stored up in the mind and body of their predecessors. Conversely, parents can also work to become consciously aware of their own childhood pain and recognize how they transmit historical violence to their children by hitting. At any rate, facts do speak for themselves. They all survived growing up and respect and parental love seems to be doing just fine. It could very well be that professional analysis, scientific advice, and studies are, to a great extent, exaggerated. Clearly, it still remains that the majority of parents claim they spank their kids. Various factors increase the likelihood too, including areas of the country they live in, their family income, race, and religion. But all in all, it's a pretty clear picture.

A lot of pediatricians and child behavior specialists continue to discourage the practice, but the truth be known, they are simply intimidated. They might even agree with physical reprimands, but they're scared to death to be seen in public as espousing corporeal authority.

When does spanking become abuse? There's an obvious overarching belief that children need to learn discipline to function in society. Spanking or a firm squeeze to the arm or neck is needed at times to forcibly teach this lesson. Trained child behavior professionals believe someone can teach those limits without physical authority. In some cases, this may be absolutely possible. If that type of guidance works, more power to them.

There's a natural instinct. All humans are inherently born with a type of self-interest defense protection. There's simply a "get" attitude. But reversing this personality is quite impossible since society sets an example. Why would it be surprising for anyone with a two-year old who thinks it is okay to hit? What is practiced is an instinct. Then comes the "upper-hand" from the child's family authority who teaches the toddler to stop whatever behavior is not good for them by developing a fear of the spanking. That's a parent's job.

There's nothing more appropriate than to stop and reflect on this. A personal account may shed some light on this basic principle. This little story is about my growing-up years. I was about 4 or 5, living in a Los Angeles suburb.

The family residence was on a typical residential paved street with concrete sidewalks, curbs and storm gutters. We lived on relatively steep grade, and car drivers were not exactly cautious. So residents were very concerned about their children's safety.

The neighborhood was new. Stucco boxes were popping up all over and families with toddlers and young children were everywhere. Back then, spanking was just a common threat. And that one huge dictate by the authoritarian figure was, "Do not step one foot on the asphalt unless I hold your hand. If I catch you, I'll give you a spanking you'll never forget."

I was one who understood consequences of even thinking about stepping out into the street. Kids sometimes lined up on their side and dared the assembly of kids on the opposite side to touch the pavement. "You better not or you'll get a spanking," some shouted.

Well, one morning a two year old boy escaped his domain. I was staring out of the front picture window and witnessed his naked butt running across the front yard heading for the street. Quickly I ran out the entry door, down some steps, and out into the front yard to scream at him.

He didn't stop. But a car came over the hill and was barreling down, heading for the danger zone. My screaming is what brought the frantic mother racing outside. Thankfully she grabbed his defiant arm about the time he was a couple of feet into the right-of-way. And it was just in time, avoiding a devastating outcome and horrible scene.

Sometimes, incidences are panic stricken episodes, fueled by threats and fear, which are beneficial for survival. This development was certainly worthy of this recognition. So there's something to learn here, though it contradicts the most basic ideas and promises from behavioral scientists.

Chapter 17: Dealing With Public Tantrums

Tantrums are every parent's nightmare, especially when in public. Almost every parent usually faces such situation, where they have to deal with the tantrums of their little ones in public. However, that doesn't mean you are a bad parent.

Every child has different reasons of throwing tantrums. We need to understand the reasons behind these tantrums which will help us to handle these without being embarrassed.

A child may throw tantrums when they are frustrated, irritated, tired or maybe they feel they are not heard and they are trying to gain your attention. Do not stop taking your child along just because you want to avoid being embarrassed. Yelling or screaming at the child won't help. In fact they are likely to get more irritated and worse and difficult to manage. Do not be embarrassed or ashamed of your child's behavior. You are not the chosen one to go through all this. Every parent has to go through this situation.

One of the biggest challenges is when you are shopping with your child. There are times when they would suddenly start bouncing up and down. They totally want to go to the toy shop nearby. You can tell them you will return once you finish shopping. But children often may get irritated if they do not like the place. If there is a play area around (now a days most of the malls have it) and you know you child can spend some time there, it would be a good idea to let them ease their frustration or boredom for a little while, it also gives you a chance to take a break and have them spend some of their abundant energy.

Involve them if you are buying something for them. If we keep them occupied there are good chances we will be able to avoid any potential tantrums and they will be fine.

It is also important you don't give in to all their demands. Just let them know firmly that if they misbehave, they will be taken back home. If the child understands, let him know you appreciate his understanding and praise him for being such a good child.

Children also throw tantrums when they are hungry or tired. Carry snacks along whenever you are stepping out. Make sure they have got enough rest before going out. If you are at the church or at doctor's clinic or any such place the best way to handle your child's tantrum is to pick your child and move out of that place taking him out of that environment to distract his mind a little bit.

Another place which you may child's tantrum are restaurants or eating joints. According to most parents almost every other child get fussy about the type of food they want. You place an order and suddenly they want something else. They will cry their heart out to get an ice cream or a candy. If their demands are not reasonable, be prepared for a tradeoff. Let them know that they can have ice cream after they eat a regular healthier meal, tell them you too want ice cream and will definitely have one after eating a regular meal. Many times they feel they want to be in control and not having it frustrates them and even infuriates the heck out of them.

However you react, and whatever actions you take are activities that the toddler sees the parents doing and will want to imitate. One of the ways to give them a feeling of control is to give them choices so that they feel they are making things happen. People may stare but that is alright. Do not give in to get away from their eyes. Tantrums may eventually fade out as the child grows because they are able to communicate better. You may find it weird initially but it you learn the tricks of the trade it will be easy to handle these situations.

Separation Anxiety

Separation Anxiety is children's way of expressing fear or discomfort about getting away from you. Every child at some point may face this. It can occur suddenly out of nowhere.

You are around your children since they are born. They are so used to seeing you around that if you get away from their sight even for a few minutes they may be restless and uneasy. It's the fear of getting away from you or losing you that creates this kind of an anxiety. It can be difficult for you to get away when your child is screaming and crying. Being a parent you cannot leave your child with teary eyes, it just breaks your heart.

There are kids who will never go to anyone else except whom they have seen around them always. They are used to seeing you around day and night. They would start crying as soon as someone unfamiliar picks them up.

Encourage them to interact with new faces. Be around to see how they react.

One of the best ways to ease some of the anxiety that your child feels as you have to leave for work for example is by gaining their trust.

During the day make plans where you may have to be away from your child for some time. Go for some shopping, go for a walk.

Spend some time away from the child. It may not be for a long time. Talk to your children. Let them know you will be back soon. If you tell them you will be back in 30 minutes, make sure you come back on time. Your kids will get used to this. You need to remember to keep their trust.

It can be a challenge to send your children to school when it is for the first time. You may have to face it for a few days till they are settled in the school and it becomes their routine.

You need to understand while in school they will be away from you for a longer period of time so they may be take some time to get adjusted. Even if they cry and make a big fuss about going to school, make sure you take them yourself the first times at least if you will regularly have someone else do it. If possible take them around the place a couple of days before and show them things that interests them. Let them see other children around. Talk to other kids in front of them. Also, it helps to not drop them off to school yourself every day. Ask other family members to drop them once in a while if possible. You can discuss with the teacher and ask them to help. When you meet them after school ask them how their day went. If you are a working parent and you leave your child with a care giver, make sure your child is comfortable. As you would be away from them for a longer period they shouldn't be restless or scared. You can help them develop hobbies so that it helps them keep their mind occupied and not start thinking about you not being around.

Your child may also be scared to stay in bed away from you at night. Make a bedtime routine for them. Make sure they are comfortable. Read out stories. You can keep a dim light on if required. Tell them you will be around.

Separation Anxiety is normal in your child's growth. However, with time it will pass. They will understand that the separation is temporary and they will come back to you.

Chapter 18: Preventions & Solutions

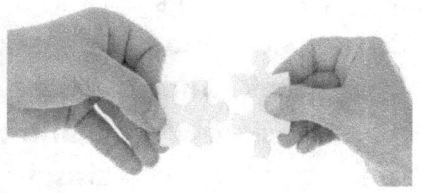

Even with all the lessons on parenting do's and don'ts, sometimes it boils down to the basic day to day behaviour of the parents. How their connection unfolds every day, what they say to the child and how they make her feel, all this combined together plays a major role in building or ruining a child's future. More often than not, everyone knows right from wrong, when it comes to parenting. The differentiating factor is actually applying it to their daily life. Most parents know what the right thing to do is. They struggle with the "how" part. To make life easier, these are some easy to understand and easy to practice behaviours.

1. Mental & Emotional Growth

Parents should treat their child as an equal, and not as someone who lacks ability or is worthless. **The child deserves respect**, and her feelings should always be taken into consideration. **She should be allowed to speak and it is of utmost importance to acknowledge and respond to what she says. Parents should respect their child's opinion.** This not only helps in building the child's confidence, but also helps her understand that it is important to respect others and be considerate towards them. Her goals and dreams are important as well. Many a times, parents observe innocence and lack of knowledge in things that their child says or does. It becomes important to give her the benefit of doubt and also understand that her understanding of things will always be a little less than theirs. **Respecting her thoughts and beliefs without disregarding them, will help with her anxiety issues and accelerate mental growth.**

2. Preserving The Innocence While Maintaining The Growth Timeline

A child is not capable of understanding and coping with grown-up problems. **Parents, at all times should maintain boundaries between their problems and children's problems. Discussions related to money, marital problems and work related stress, should not be held in front of the child.** Her innocence should be protected at all times and she should be allowed to remain a child till the time her mind develops significantly to understand the intensity of grown-up problems. Dealing with age appropriate problems, helps the child to figure out her coping mechanism. This helps her grow into an independent adult who is also emotionally stable.

3. Parenting ≠ Financial Support

Parents should not relate parenting to merely providing for another human being or providing financial support. It is important to understand that a child does not understand the parents' actions in terms of money. For her love is not measured with number of things they buy for her. She understands the attention she gets and the time that is spent with her doing things she loves. This helps her realise her worth and builds up her self-esteem. Some parents believe that children see them as cheque books although this belief is plain wrong. Giving her what she asks for all the time, showering her with gifts and rewarding her every time she accomplishes something, is not the best thing to do. In fact it's not appropriate at all. Rewarding her in kind and providing for her in kind, leads her to believe that she can have everything without being aware of the hard work it takes to acquire those things. It is also important that parents understand that it is motivation that will keep their child going. No amount of rewards or gifts will surpass the value of **parents who are supporting and who appreciate their child at every step.**

4. Parental Love And Warmth ≠ A Deal, Also, Not Negotiable

Parents should not make their child work hard for parental warmth and love. It is important for parents to love their child unconditionally. Making her fight for acceptance and love, by expecting flawless performance at school or at a sport is not the right way to parent a child. This will lead her into believing that love is measured by success and she will lack compassion. It is important to let the child know when she is doing something wrong or when something is not good for her. It is important to remember that constant criticism and no appreciation leads the child to lose self-belief and also distances her from her parents. The most effective way of doing so is by appreciating her when she does well or makes an intelligent decision. **A balance of both criticism and appreciation, makes her believe that her actions are acknowledged and the strength of her relationship with her parents is not solely based on her performance.**

5. Introducing Failure As A Natural Outcome And Building Motivation

Parents who have a habit of overreacting and berating their child when she fails or performs badly at a certain thing, lead her into believing that it is better to lie to them to stay in their good books. They should resort to appreciating her and they should also constantly motivate their child by telling her that putting efforts and not giving up in the face of failure is the best way to live by. **This will not only** build her confidence **but also** help her cope with failure **in a better manner.** The child should be made aware of the fact that failure is not a bad thing. She should be made to believe that failure is acceptable and her relation with the parents is not affected by failure. **This helps in keeping extreme thoughts like, suicide and self-harm, at bay. It also results in development of her ability to cope with failure.**

6. Responsibility and Self-learning

It is important to trust the child with small tasks at home. It could as simple as a household chore like setting up the dinner table or picking out her outfit for the day, etc. This gives her a sense of responsibility and also a chance to learn on her own. **Constantly doing things for the child and micro-managing her**, leads to lack of confidence in her and also decelerates her development process. Time and again parents should take a step back, and let their child grow a little on her own. This does not mean that they should be completely uninvolved, it just means that they **should allow the child to do certain things on her own and let her figure a way out of her problems**. This not only **gives the child a sense of responsibility** but also helps her feel like a grown-up. It reinstates the feeling that she is important and her freedom is valued.

7. Behaviour-check and reaction-control

Having a child around means that parents should always keep a check on their own behaviour. The best way to do so is to take a moment to decide if they would like to see their child behave in the manner that they behave or react in a manner similar to theirs. A child follows her parents in terms of reactions and behaviour. What she sees is subconsciously picked by her brain. So parents who often complain of their child's behaviour should address the problem at its root. They should start by **treating each other with respect, especially in the presence of their child.They should also not misbehave with anyone around them either.** It is important for the child to understand that discrimination based on any factor is not acceptable and everyone is an equal. This teaches her to treat everyone with equal respect and not to be rude to anyone.

8. Rationalizing the NO

When children start lying and start showing signs of secrecy, parents should try and be reasonable. More often than not, constantly saying no to the child leads her to question her self-worth and she starts hiding things. To avoid such behaviour, **parents should offer another solution and give valid reasons for denying her request.** This not only **develops her rationale** but also helps her believe that parents have her best interest in mind. This also **helps in building trust in the relationship. Parents should keep a check on their reactions. Extreme reaction to anything that the child does, makes the child distant and nervous.** A child who constantly lives in fear, develops anxiety issues. Her secretive behaviour makes it worse. As a result of it, most of the times parents stay unaware of the bigger problems due to her secretive nature. The child develops trust issues. Such children not only are emotionally unstable but also become victims of depression as a result of dealing with everything on their own.

9. Quality time = Quality bonding

Parents should make time for their child and give her attention. Parents who have a busy work life, **should make time for their child** while doing things that they usually do. For example, when reading a book, parents can involve the child by letting her also read an age-appropriate book next to them. Parents who unwind by playing a certain sport can involve their child by teaching them the same sport.

This not only helps them spend time with their child but also helps teach her a new activity. This **makes the child feel wanted and parental attention builds her self-esteem.**

10. Follow what you Preach

Parents whose child has difficulty in accepting her mistakes, should address the problem by leading with example. **They should start accepting their own mistakes in front of the child.** This not only **teaches her to be humble but also makes her believe that making mistakes and accepting them is okay**. The child should be made to understand that it's important to learn from the mistake and making a mistake is natural.

Seeking External Help

And when all falls weak, when parents start believing that the damage is beyond repair, they should not fall prey to that feeling. Sometimes, even after trying everything, parents don't see the expected results. In such cases, some parents resort to old ways, some lose patience and give up, and some totally distance themselves from their child. At such times, they should seek external help.

Seeking help from a 3rd person is not a sign of weakness or failure. Some parents refrain from it because they see it as an embarrassment. As long as this belief is not changed, the damage will keep increasing.

There are quite a few options available, once the parents start looking around for help. When deciding to seek help it is important for parents to have answers to these question. This helps in narrowing down to the context of the problem and the particular area or member that needs help.

- What is the particular parenting challenge that they face?
- Is there more than one challenge?
- How and what is it affecting? For e.g. their behaviour, their relationship with the spouse, their relationship with the child, the child's behaviour, the child's mental or physical growth, or the relationship between the whole family.

Once there is clarity and parents have the answers to these questions, parents should go ahead and seek appropriate counsel. Few of the many options available today are, overall mental health counselling, family counselling, marriage counselling, child development counselling etc.

If parents do not feel comfortable talking to someone they don't know, and find it difficult to trust a counsellor, they should not give up the idea of seeking help from a 3rd person altogether. In such cases it is advisable to talk to a close friend, their own parents or someone they look up to.

Sometimes a 3rd person's perspective is all that is needed.

Chapter 19: The Contributions Of Dad

Single parenting has been widely accepted over the past several decades.As a phenomenon that continually grows, like so many other social changes, society is forced to accept that single parenting is here to stay, and we need to embrace that reality.There are so many that lobby value of single parenting that the defensiveness causes many to overlook the negative affect that single parenting has on the kids.It is however, irresponsible at all levels to avoid looking at those statistics and push a personal agenda through so we can satisfy a group of people. We need to focus on the children and kids will be experiencing as a result of being raised in a single parent environment.These elements need to be thoroughly examined and taken seriously.It cannot be what the parents "think" are best for the children; it has to be what "is" best for the children.However, these lines are easily blurred when that decision needs to be made.

There is an undeniable fact that kids thrive and become more healthy adults when raised in two parent environments — a mother, and a father.But identities contributed components that are key in raising children.A mother cannot meet the needs a child needs to have met by their father, and vice versa — both parents are equally important.

Unfortunately, however, we live in a society of "dead beat dads" or many single parents have been put into their role without say — those are the very unfortunate circumstances that are unfair.However, young women that become pregnant and entertain the idea of going at it alone do not understand the bigger picture for their kids.Choices are made, some good, and some bad, but when a choice to raise a child as a single parent is decided, there is often lack of consideration for the child.

A father brings to parenting so much that a mother cannot bring.Each parent has a different way of identifying to the child and disciplining the child, neither better, but both needed.Statistics have shown that having a loving and nurturing father is vital for a child's happiness, social and academic success.These same statistics exist for having a mother.In addition, the father or mother's absence from the children's lives greatly influences emotional instability, lack of self-esteem, depression, and social withdrawal and aggression levels.

Studies have shown that a father plays a large role in the shaping of a young girl's self-esteem.A young girl self-esteem and emotional state is greatly influenced by her father. Young girls and teens need to receive reassurance from their fathers that they are important, valued and beautiful.This cannot just happen when they are younger but is needed throughout the formative years and adolescent years of their lives.When a daughter receives affirmation from her father, she is more self-confident, adjusted and able to maintain healthy relationships.Absent of this, a girl has trouble not only with her esteem, but loving herself.

A father brings to sons direction and can teach them how to become a man.Of course there are "bad" fathers that live in homes, however, a father that is dedicated to being a leader, raising boys to men significantly alters the course of a young boy's life.A woman cannot teach a boy how to be a man.

Households with both a mom and a dad present provide more stability and balance and create an environment and dynamic that is healthy for a child to grow.The fundamentals that both parents contribute cannot be viewed as insignificant.Single parenting is a bad approach no matter what parent is doing the child rearing.Children, kids and teens need both parents.

Chapter 20: How To Get More Involved In

Your Child's Education

A child's education begins at home, but parental involvement doesn't end when that child steps through the school door. Studies show that children not only do better in school when their parents are involved, they also tend to go further in the education system.

To help you stay connected while your child is in class, many school systems are using a highspeed notification and response service called the Immediate Response Information System, or IRIS.

Developed by Tech Radium Inc., IRIS sends routine, priority and emergency messages electronically from school to parents, guardians and emergency responders. These messages which range from informing you of your child's attendance record and grades to alerting you of early school closures due to inclement weather - are sent to home and cell phones, e-mail accounts, pagers, fax machines and PDAs.

Though better communication between school and home is one way parents can become more involved, the following tips offer further ways parents can participate in their children's education:

* Talk regularly. Whether it's at dinner or during the drive home from school, ask your child questions about the school day and about homework assignments.

* Help your child practice good study habits. Create a
quiet, clutter-free study space. If homework help is needed, assist with the work but don't do it for your child.

* Get suggestions from teachers. If your child is having trouble in a subject or is displaying behavioral problems, arrange a meeting with your child's teacher to discuss the matter and possible solutions.

* Attend meetings. You can learn about new and pending school policies at school board meetings. PTA meetings also can provide aid and support for parents.

How To Get Your Toddler To Eat Well

Toddlers are notoriously picky eaters. Not a parent exists that hasn't worried about their toddlers eating habits at one time or another.

Some worry their toddlers aren't eating enough, others worry that their toddlers are eating too much, and still others worry that their toddlers aren't eating a wide enough variety of different foods.

The good news is that if you do things right, you can set your toddler on a path to good eating indefinitely.

How do you do it?

First and foremost, know that when it comes to eating most toddlers are just learning about food, and just starting to develop habits.

You don't want to force food on your toddler at any time, or suggest that they clean their plate or take just one last bite of anything.

Why? This may set them up for a lifetime of food struggles.

Rather, the best way to support good eating habits is to have available at all times a variety of healthy foods in your home.

Generally as long as toddlers eat one or two items from each food group within a 2-3 day time frame, they are doing well.

Here are some other things you can do to encourage healthy eating habits: Eat as a Family – This may not be possible every day of the week, but at least 1-2 days per week you should encourage your family to gather together around the table for a good, wholesome meal. Include lots of different foods that are healthy and nutritious. Toddlers learn by example, and watching other family members eat and interact in an inviting environment will encourage your toddler to do the same as time goes on.

Don't Require Your Toddler to Clean His Plate – This is a common well intentioned mistake some parents make. Toddlers eating habits are peculiar, but they do know when they are hungry. Forcing them to finish food they can't or won't eat will only result in power struggles and potentially problems with food later in life.

Keep the Refrigerator Stocked with Healthy Snacks – If you don't have dozens of cookies laying about the house your toddler will be less likely to eat them. That said allow your toddler some sweet treats when they are visiting relatives or a friend's house. Just remember to keep sweets to a minimum at your house.

Cook a Variety of Foods – If you normally cook fish twice a week, your child will become accustomed to it as part of their routine.

It will be much easier to convince your toddler to try new things if they are an ordinary part of your diet, then if out of the blue you decide to try new foods that are unusual or generally unappealing.

As your toddler grows and develops they will eventually develop more routine eating habits. In the meantime simply providing healthy alternatives and variety in their diet is a great way to jump start a healthy diet.

How to Help Your Kids Succeed In School All Year

Research shows that parental involvement in schools improves student achievement, reduces absenteeism and restores confidence among parents in their children's education.

"Children need parents who have an interest in what's going on in the classroom," said Reg Weaver, president of the National Education Association. "Parents must do everything they can to get their children fully engaged at school, reinforce their learning at home and develop a strong relationship with their teachers."

NEA, the nation's largest educators organization, offers the following tips for parents on how they can ensure a successful educational experience for their children:

*Go to parent-teacher conferences. If the school doesn't have them, set aside a time to meet with your children's teachers. Ask how your children are doing and review their work. Let the teachers know how and when it is best to reach you. Finally, ask how you can support your children's learning at home.

*Visit the classrooms. Getting a firsthand look at what is going on in your children's classrooms will help you stay informed about what they are learning at school.

*Join the PTA or other parent group. Go to school events, such as back-to-school night. As a group, parents can help schools reach their goals.

*Pay attention to what your children are learning at school. Be aware of what they need to know to meet the standards set for their grade level.

*Contact the school if you have any concerns. Parental involvement also means reading to your children, checking homework every night, limiting television viewing on school nights or simply asking your children about their school day.

"Whatever your level of involvement, do it consistently and regularly because it will make an important difference in your children's lives," Weaver said.

How To Motivate A Child

I have two children and even though I love them to bits, I have to say that at times they need motivating to do their homework or to help out around the house, for example. This article describes how I go about this child motivation. The methods have helped my own children no end and I am sure they could help other parents in a similar situation.

I remember when I met my step-daughter who is called Taryn. She was five years of age and quite a character. I felt a bit sorry for her however as she spent a lot of time at a childminders. The child minder would take her and pick her up from school. On some days her mother would not be able to collect her until around 8pm.

After a few months of dating her mother, I offered to help out by stating that I could take Taryn to school and pick her up. Taryn said that she wanted me to do this and it was all agreed.

Up to this point Taryn had never really been made to do her homework, either by her mother who was very busy and often tired or by the child minder.

When we arrived home from school on the first day of me picking her up, I asked Taryn if she had any homework. She passed me her reading folder. In the folder was a book which she was supposed to read. Come on then Taryn lets read this book together, I said. I don't do homework, Taryn replied. I stated to her that that was the past and that from now on she would be doing it.

Taryn had a bit of strop and started to cry. Your not my dad, you can not make me do it, she continued. I basically had to be very strong and made her read the book. There were a number of words which she could not read and I wrote them on a list. We then spent around ten minutes where I attempted to teach her the words. She found all of this very boring.

I then told her that we would now play a game, which is called the mouthing game. She would pick a word from the list and just mouth the word without making a sound. If I could guess what she had mouthed, she would get a point and then it would be my turn.

Taryn really enjoyed this game and on the way home from school on the next day, she asked if we could play the game again. Of course we can but we need to read the book first, I said. Taryn replied that this was fine. This is one example of many games we play when doing homework or any other task which the children see as mundane.

I also compliment both children and tell them how much I love and am proud of them at regular intervals. I give them rewards when they have a good school report and encourage them to always give things ago even if they believe that they might fail in the specific task. In my opinion there is no such thing as failure if

Chapter 21: Get Active

It can be so very tough, when you're in a dark place, to think of ways that you can get active. Make a list now of things that are generally accessible to you that you know make you feel better. You'll use this list later to create a checklist.

Introspection

Allow yourself time for introspection.

I know during those dark days, I might prefer not to stop to think, not to examine my thoughts, usually because I am afraid of what I might find there.

This isn't helpful.

You need to allow yourself **time to think.** Whether it happens while you're washing the dishes, or if you're able to have a warm bath, or spend an hour in the gym, turn off the music, put down the books, don't watch the TV. Just allow yourself time to mull things over in your mind. At first it can actually physically hurt, but allow yourself to break through.

If you can ask yourself 'why', you might find some answers.

Hold a conversation with yourself. Be compassionate with yourself too. For example:

"Why am I feeling this way today?"

My mother died.

Yes, but she didn't die today. Why am I feeling this way today.

Because it's her birthday next week and I can't think for the pain of missing her. It catches in my chest.

Okay. Now we know why we're feeling this way. It's okay to feel this way, I'm allowed to feel.

What can I do about it?

Can I show the kids some pictures of their grandmother? Can we talk about her? Will that help me?

Maybe I can write her a letter? Maybe I can take the kids to the park and sit in the sun and write her a letter she'll never read, but I can tell her all the things I wish I had told her.

Good ideas, all.

I have acknowledged that I feel sad. I have identified why I feel sad. I have categorised this sadness as something I can do something about today. I have thought of something I can do about it. Now I just need to do it.

Allow yourself the opportunity to know yourself. You might just be surprised by what you find. In the immortal words of Winnie the Pooh, "**You are braver than you believe, stronger than you seem, and smarter than you think."**

Activity 6: Introspection

What are some of the questions you could ask yourself when you're struggling? Write them down now to remind you when you need them.

Identify your triggers

This is once again about allowing yourself to know yourself.

What are the things that make a bad day a horrible day? For me it's having to moan, yell and cajole my children into being subservient little beings who sit quietly in a corner colouring while I mope about all day. That never works out for me.

My children don't know how to be quiet, and they are certainly not subservient little beings, and in truth I wouldn't really ever want them to be.

So here I am, having a bad day, feeling like I can't breathe for the pressure on me, and my kids.... are too loud? Are too excitable? Won't clean up the mess they made?

And I explode.

And I say things I don't mean.

And I say mean things I'm ashamed of myself for.

Why? Because I can't cope. I'm not coping.

I know my children. I know they don't like sitting watching TV all day. More importantly, I know it's not good for them. I know that they're going to be hungry when they wake up, and if I don't have something for them to snack on they'll help themselves. I know they'll want lunch around 1pm and I know they'll start asking for dinner around 5.30pm. I know if they're not ready for bed by around 7pm, they start getting ratty and refusing to go to bed. These are known factors.

If I choose to lie in bed and let them get their own breakfast, I must anticipate milk on the floor. My children are small. I can't expect them not to spill the heavy milk. If I don't make them something to eat, they will try to help me by making something themselves, and I will be left with not only the cleaning up but the waste too. And because I'm unhappy, I will moan at them.

By identifying your trigger, you can prevent the behaviours that trip them.

If I put cereal out the night before, and pour the right amount of milk into their drinks bottles, they can make their own breakfast in the morning without making a mess.

If I have sufficient snacks available when I know they will be hungry, they don't have to nag for it. If I can plan a walk to the park, or a play date, or just a dig around on the beach for a part of the day, it prevents their whining, bickering and boredom before it has a chance to start, and I help myself in the process.

Do you know how hard it is to drag myself to the park when I can barely drag myself out of bed?

Yes, I do. But remember, we're **choosing** to cope. The agony of dragging yourself out the front door isn't that much more than the agony of having raged through the house like a flaming banshee, the guilt of feeling like you're failing as a parent, and the unchanged state of mind, coupled with now hurting and resentful children.

Chapter 22: Use Supplements To

Maintain Your Children's Health Naturally

Sometimes, no matter how well we think we eat, there are nutritional gaps that need to be filled so that we can feel completely healthy, energized every day, and strong. The same goes for our children, especially if our children are picky eaters or are sick. Teach your children at a young age to enjoy taking supplements that will boost their health and prevent illness, so they can take these good habits into adulthood.

Gummy multi-vitamin/mineral supplements are the best way to introduce young children to taking supplements for health. Tell your children that these supplements are to be taken in addition to the healthy foods they eat, so that if they are not getting enough of a particular nutrient from their diet that day, the supplement will fill in the gap and make their bodies grow strong.Once a child is old enough to swallow pills, he/she can learn to take the supplement in that form instead of in the gummy form.In the meantime, though, gummy vitamins are flavorful and are more like a snack than a supplement.

Just like gummy vitamins, there are children's vitamins that come in chewable tablet form.These are just as effective and just as tasty, but their texture is different from the gummy texture, so it is up to your child which type of chewable supplement he/she would prefer to take daily.

You can also entice children to take their supplements by telling them that the vitamins and minerals prevent illness, making it less likely that they will have to see the doctor, someone whom many children are afraid of visiting.

Note that children who have a varied diet of home-prepared vegetables and fruits may not necessarily need additional supplements. However, when such children get sick, it may be beneficial to aid their recovery and/or general well-being by letting them take a suitable supplement (for example a general children's one-a-day multi-vitamin) for a set period of time (for example; 1 month).

Ways to Teach Children to be Safe during Physical Activities and Sports

Whenever children participate in any kind of physical activity, whether it is playing on a sports team or in a gym class at school, as well as riding a bicycle, running, or exercising, there is the risk of injury.Even riding as a passenger in a car can pose a threat of injury if an accident were to occur.Parents need to teach their children about the inherent dangers in every physical activity, from skateboarding and rollerblading to swimming, gymnastics, and dance.

The best way to teach your children about safety procedures is to start teaching them while they are young.For example, teach your child to not run while holding anything in his/her mouth or hands, as a fall can result in serious injury.Or teach your child that if he/she is going to go rollerblading, he/she must first learn how to do it properly in a confined, safe area rather than jumping right into rollerblading down the streets in your neighborhood.Just like using parent supervision and floatation devices prior to learning how to swim, or training wheels before learning how to ride a bike on two wheels, children need to understand that they need to learn slowly when it comes to physical activities that can lead to injury if not executed properly.And they should be taught to wear protective gear, such as helmets and pads.

When it comes to riding in cars, make sure to teach your children the importance of using a safety belt (assuming your child is old enough to use a safety belt directly instead of a baby/child or booster seat) and for example keeping their arms inside the vehicle.The sooner they get into the routine of snapping on that seatbelt as soon as they get into the seat of a car, the easier it will be for them to remember to do so even if they are riding with someone other than their parents.

There are many more precautions that need to be taken with and for children on a daily basis. A good commonsense thinking approach, aided by information obtained from government organizations, schools, youth/child organizations, and even the Internet will help you to keep your child safe during physical activities and sports.

Chapter 23: How To Talk To Your Teen

One of the hardest things that you may need to do with your teen is to talk to them. While you should maintain open communication throughout their lives, it is especially important to have a conversation if you feel like something is going on with them. Whether you are worried about thoughts of suicide, depression, or addiction, you need to be there and ready to talk through the issue with your teen.

This is a hard time to deal with your children. You may be worried about sounding too judgmental and like you are blaming them for the issues at hand. But you need to be open and ready to hear what they have to say. Be aware that this is going to be hard to handle sometimes. You may not like to hear what they have to say. But if you sit back, show your support, and discuss the issues with them, it becomes much easier to get them to open up and find them the help that they may need if one of these issues is present.

Actively Listen

Your child is not going to respond well to you if they feel like they are being judged in the process. You need to sit back and actually listen to them and show that you understand. If you are worried about what you are going to yell at the teen about or blame them for doing something stupid, they are going to clam up and not want to tell you a thing. Rather, you need to practice doing some active listening.

This is a type of listening that a lot of people just don't know how to use on a daily basis. They are too busy worrying about what they need to say rather than listening to what they are being told. To do this, you need to listen to what your teen is saying, use the right body language to show that you are listening, and even summarize what the other person is saying to make sure that you understand what they are saying. This shows the teen that you are interested in listening to them and what they have to say, no matter how hard the topic.

Don't Freak Out

This is going to be a hard one to do if your child is explaining that they feel depressed, are dealing with an addiction, or they are going through thoughts of suicide. No parent wants to hear that their little one is dealing with such grown up issues. But if you freak out as a first reaction, your child is going to feel like something is wrong with them and that you have stopped listening. The teen is not going to want to talk anymore and you could effectively close up the lines of communication. It is much better if you are able to stay calm. Even if you are freaking out inside, stay calm and listen to what your teen is telling you, taking the issues seriously and affirming the feelings that your teen is telling you. These actions show your teen that you can handle what they are telling you and that you would like to be there to help them out.

Ask Questions

Sometimes your teen is going to be slow at coming out with the information. But they did start out with the information so they are ready to talk, they just may not be sure about how to continue on with the information. If they have started to talk but you have very little idea about the severity of the issue, take the time to ask some questions. For example, when it comes to your child admitting that they think about suicide, you can ask them what they mean when they talk about suicide and how often they feel like this. When you ask questions, you become better equipped to deal with the situation because you know what is going on and how to deal with the whole deal.

Give the Teen Some Input

When it comes to getting your teen the help that they need, let them have some of the input. They were willing to come to you for someone to talk to and for some help, so they should get some say in the treatment that they get. When they get a bit of say into the whole thing, you are going to find that it is much easier to get them to go through the treatment and finish it. But when you force them to go into treatment, you will see that they are going to be more rebellious and may not even finish it out.

There are a variety of different things that you can do for treatment. If they are dealing with the depressive issues, you will need to get them to a psychologist who will help them to find the right treatment, perhaps medication and talking out the issues a bit more. Those who are suffering from addiction may have to go through some kind of detox treatment. But when the two of you, or more if you would like to include some other family members for support, decide on what to do together, it is much easier to get through this process and see the right end that you would like.

Be Supportive

The most important thing that you can do through this process is to be supportive. Your child has come to you; there are many teenagers who would assume that their parents don't understand and won't even try to approach their parents for some help. But since they did come to you and are willing to admit that there is an issue, take this into consideration and realize how hard it was for them to come and talk to you.

Many parents will spend too much time making judgments and jumping down the throats of their children. They may feel like the teenager made a horrible mistake and should have been better. They may feel that the teenager should have listened to them and that things should have gone in a different manner. But jumping to conclusions is not the right step.

Yes, your teenager should not have taken the drugs or be thinking about suicide, but this is why they are trying to get some help. They realize that there is something wrong with this and they are asking for help. If you jump at them and start accusing or making them feel bad, you are going to end up with a teenager who withdraws and won't talk to you any longer.

Save the accusations and the jumping for later on. Your teenager is going to feel bad enough as it is. It is better to be supportive, and thankful, that they came to you in the first place. Focus on helping them out as much as you can, and ignore any of the crazy thoughts that are going through your head. Help them to get their treatment or any help that is needed and worry about the rest later. It does not matter how bad the decision might have been originally, that is done with at this point. Rather, it is much better to take care of the situation as your child knows there is an issue at hand already, and then worry about the rest later.

Dealing with your child having an issue, whether it is an addiction, depression, or thoughts of suicide are never easy. It is much better to worry about talking with your child about these issues and learning how to deal with them so your teenager is able to get the help that they need as soon as possible.

Chapter 24: What Not To Do And Why

All of us make mistakes when it comes to discipline – there is no getting around it and oftentimes that is how we learn how to be better parents. When it comes to setting rules and enforcing them, it can be a bit difficult when you have a headstrong three-year-old that is not willing to budge and throws a tantrum every time he or she does not get their way.

Many times parents lose control of themselves while trying to discipline their children because we want to teach our children right from wrong and many times we become frustrated.Oftentimes, parents feel bad about the way they have disciplined their children after the fact, and this often leads parents to forego disciplining in the future. No matter how good our intentions are, we are going to make mistakes, but in this chapter I want to go over the most common mistakes that are made by parents when it comes to disciplining.

1.Parents often lose their temper when it comes to disciplining their children; you have to make sure not to do this. Many times parents become stressed out from having to repeat themselves over and over again. This leads to children getting disciplined out of anger; things are said that can lead to hurt feelings, and the child can feel shamed. This type of behavior teaches a child that screaming and losing control of yourself is okay in a relationship. Instead, take some time to relax before you begin disciplining the child; ensure that you correct him in a loving manner.

2.Physical punishment is another mistake that many parents make. Often times the parents try to justify this behavior by saying "Spare the rod, spoil the child", but this is a temporary solution that only teaches that hitting and hurting others is acceptable. Children who are punished physically tend to display the same behavior when it comes to other children, meaning that when they get angry, they hit. Instead, find a different way to discipline the child.

3. Bribery is something that many of us turn to when we are in public and want our children to behave. Most of us are guilty of offering a treat if only the child will behave while in public. Bribes are a quick fix. They are going to get you the peace you want at that moment, but you are setting yourself up for future issues. Instead, try rewarding good behavior. Don't bribe the child, but when he or she does something good, that is when to give them a reward. This will reinforce the good behavior.

4. One thing that can drive a child crazy is lecturing. Take it from someone that listened to their fair share of lectures growing up – nothing that you are saying is sticking. The child is not listening to you and is focused on how annoyed he is. He will become resentful, and oftentimes simply get sick of listening to you speak. Instead, explain why the behavior was wrong, discipline the child, and move on.

5. Many parents also think that threats will work when it comes to trying to get their children to behave. That is true for a very short period of time. When the child realizes that you are not going to follow through, your threats do not scare the child into behaving any longer and he learns that you do not do what you say you will do. This means he loses trust in you. Instead, say what you mean and mean what you say. Follow through and don't just threaten to discipline your child.

Don't beat yourself up if you have made these mistakes in the past and don't worry about it if you make them in the future. Be aware of the mistake, learn from it, and move on. Everyone makes mistakes in life, and in parenting the most important thing that you can do is learn from your mistakes.

Chapter 25: How To Praise Your Toddler

The Right Way

One of the great things about being a parent is watching them succeed. You can't help but to feel overjoyed and feel as if you're doing something right. The last thing you want to do is neglect to provide them with the proper amount of praise. Toddlers, because of their young age, are extremely impressionable (especially as it pertains to their relationship with their parents). So how do you know what the appropriate level of praise is? You don't want to overdo it and risk spoiling your toddler, but you don't want to under do it either. This chapter will focus on some of the basic do's and don'ts in regards to praising your toddler.

Do These When Praising Your Toddler

One of the best ways to praise your toddler is to use as much positive physical emotion as possible. To do this effectively, simply pat your toddler on the shoulder, or give them a joyful hug. Some parents have found that the best way to praise their toddler is by giving them high fives or rapidly kissing them. These are all positive attributions that your toddler will take with enthusiasm. Of course, depending on your child, you might want to do something different such as giving them a thumbs up or smiling at them. The point is that your toddler will pick up on positive body language fairly quickly. Besides, actions really do speak louder than words.

Don't try to fake it; try to be as genuine as possible. This is definitely easier said than done. If you have a well rounded toddler who is always asking for praise, it can become monotonous. But try your best not to make it show. Although they're young, toddlers know when you don't really mean it. When you go to give them praise, be as specific as you can. For example, be sure that your tone of voice directly reflects your body language. When you go to give them praise, tell them exactly what they did that you thoroughly liked, and look them in the eyes when you do so. This way they'll pick up on the fact that you genuinely enjoyed what they did, and perhaps they'll do it again.

Make your praise as personal as you can. This should be the easiest to do. Many parents make comments such as "I needed this" or "I really liked that," but saying those things actually directs the attention to yourself instead of your toddler's accomplishment. Instead of saying things like that, say things like "You have been such a good boy this morning!", "Good job on finishing all of your breakfast!", "I'm so proud of you for picking up your toys!", and "You worked so hard on drawing that picture!" The rule of thumb is to use "you" more than "I". Make it all about praising your child rather than expressing your personal feelings or thoughts. Following these three rules will help you effectively praise your toddler and will ultimately cause your toddler to do them time and time again.

Don't Do These When Praising Your Toddler

Be Wary Of Over Praising Your Toddler

We mentioned it a little bit above, but over praising your toddler too much can have detrimental results. One way to over praise your toddler is by praising them for everything they do good. They'll start to expect satisfaction and pleasure every time. In order to avoid this, only praise your toddler the first few times that they do something. For example, if they eat all of their vegetables for dinner, praise them. If they do it again the next time, praise them again. But stop there. You don't want it to lose its effectiveness on other things.

Do Not Make the Praise about Your Toddler's Overall Character

It's easy to turn the praise around and make it about your toddler's character when it's supposed to be about their behavior. Saying things like "You're such a good girl", "You're the best child", or "You are not good" is simply reflecting on who they are as a person. Try your best to avoid comments like this. Instead, comment on their action by saying "You've really behaved yourself today", "You've been really good this afternoon", or "Leaving your toys on the floor was bad". This will make your toddler feel as if they have a choice to change. When you comment on who they are, they feel as if that's more of a permanent characteristic.

It's Not Critical, So Don't Make It That Way

Praise loses its intended purpose if you mix it with criticism. In many ways, this actually pushes your toddler away from you. For example, saying things like "You did really good eating your vegetables tonight, but try to be faster next time" ruins the praise altogether. It's understandable that parents think they're helping build their toddler up by doing this, but in reality it's only putting them down. Your toddler will think that they actually didn't do goo at all because they aren't receiving genuine praise from you. You should be happy enough that they actually finished their food in the first place. A creative way to establish authentic praise is to turn to somebody else in the room and say "He finished all of his vegetables last night, isn't that great?" So long as your toddler heard you, they'll be overjoyed with excitement.

Don't fall into a routine. Be intentional with your praise, and remember not to over emphasis one particular behavior. Now that you know the basic do's and don'ts about how to praise your toddler, try a few today! You'll be surprised at how easy they are, and especially how rewarding it can be for both you and your toddler. While you might need to alter the rules a bit to accommodate your child try to abide as closely as you can to these. More importantly, use praise as a way to establish a close relationship at an early age.

Chapter 26: Techno Teen

Parenting issues of the early part of the 21st Century are fraught with the difficulties of two separate and distinct skill sets:

Teenagers are able to handle a formidable array of gizmos and electronic gadgets without the slightest difficulty while the older generation struggle to find the power button!

Having no computer skills is a real handicap when it comes to supervising a teenager. Kids can present one face to the family and quite another to the online world, which incidentally is liberally populated with armies of perverts and weirdos...You would not dream of allowing your teenager to socialise at a party or disco with someone who survives on a daily diet of booze, sex drugs and alcohol yet they could be doing exactly that online and on a regular basis, right under your nose.

The mobile phone has become a 'must-have' item for teenagers and most teens are enviably knowledgeable and dextrous.They can text at the speed of lightning, fingers flying across the tiniest of keys, achieving entire conversations before you can say 'Apple!'

The mobile is a duel-edged sword for parents.It is a security lifeline that allows you to communicate with your kids wherever they are, even while they are actually en route between locations – you know exactly who they are with, where they are, how long it is going to take them to get there and when they are coming home.It has become parents' second pair of eyes and ears and few mums would consider not preventing their child from owning one.However, as with all good things there are drawbacks.

Smartphones (and computers) are a great platform for bullying.If your kid is being bullied it is likely that online social networks are being used to intimidate and threaten.Should you notice your teenager has become withdrawn or secretive a gentle discussion might reveal that he or she is being bullied or menaced in some way: if the perpetrators are based at school and the communications can be traced to school time you have somewhere to start...If not then you could try confronting parents politely – if that fails, there are avenues of help to explore such as church groups, youth groups, community help groups and as a last resort, the legal system that includes solicitors and police.

Social networking sites represent huge communities of 'friends' that swap personal information and photographs.It is a good thing to instil at an early age that online relationships are like any other – they can turn sour.Friendships that 'go bad' online can morph into vicious hate-mail episodes that are played out in the most public manner.A little reserve is a good thing when it comes to conducting online friendships – advise your teenager to choose carefully when deciding whether to share personal information with strangers they have only met electronically.

Learning How to Live

Teenagers are on the brink of leaving the nest to make their own lives, either to attend university or find jobs or get married and settle down early in life.For many it is a painful learning curve as they have received no previous grounding in life skills.

The finest gift you can give your teenager is to teach him (or her) how to live well.Living well does not necessarily mean having everything you did not have as a young adult.

Youngsters do not need the latest model of whatever four-wheel-drive is fashionable: they do need to be able to drive a car as it is a basic 'life skill'.As soon as your kid is old enough, start driving lessons.And teach not only the practical side of driving but also a code of behaviour on the public roads along with a decent grounding in the cost of insurance and maintenance etc.It is so easy to just pay the bill (if you have enough yourself that is!) on insurance and the hundred other expenses that come with being independently mobile.Teaching a teen to be responsible on the road is so much harder but they will be safer out there in the long run.

Along with teaching the basics of driving remember to include tips on how to be safe once out of the car, especially for young girls.Deserted multi-storey car parks late at night should be avoided whenever possible; the dangers of drinking and driving; what to do if you break down on a busy motorway; what to do in an accident.All of these things are vital but few parents go over them with their kids.

Balancing a cheque book is another area where most parents imagine their kids develop skills instinctively.How can you expect your nineteen-year-old to understand how to handle money responsibly if you never taught her (or him) the ins and outs of a bank statement; the difference between Checking Accounts and Savings Accounts; bank charges; interest rates; direct debits...Young teenagers are offered loans at extortionate lending rates every day — teach your teen why he should refuse them.

Paying bills is a baptism of fire for most teenagers once they leave home to start university or share with others. A simple session at home around the kitchen table with utility bills will help to ease the confusion and could prevent a whole lot of aggravation later on.

Skills are learned along the way throughout the teen years. Many mums continue to wash their teenagers' clothes right up until they leave home for a very good reason — they value their washing machine! Washing machines are expensive and teenagers are notoriously forgetful about leaving pens, lighters, coins and mobile phones in jeans pockets leading to expensive repairs. Even if you prefer your kids to leave your machine alone at least make an effort to show them how to separate wash so that it doesn't get ruined! Most university students return home for their first vacation break with a bagful of grey clothes and this is why!

Chapter 27: How To Ensure Your Child

Makes Good Choices

To ensure your child makes good choices is accomplished by starting them in the right direction at an early age. This will lay the foundation for making the right choices early on that will carry on through their school years as well into adulthood.

As good parents we must remain firm with our guidance for our kids and they must learn to obey and follow what we have defined for them. We need to convey with kindness the explanations needed to understand the general parameters we have laid down.

You must establish and maintain goodcommunication with your kids that is done on a regular basis. Let them know whether you approve or disapprove of their actions or what they say. This establishes what type of values you want them to embrace and understand. Depending on their environment these values can be validated or rejected based on what they absorb from their peers or teachers at school. The biggest thing you do not want to happen is to let any inconsistency creep into their daily lives.

A virtue your child needs to embrace is being sincere and to always tell the truth without hesitation. You need to instill in them to help other family members or people they love improve their lives when they are called upon to do so. This also will make them have more confidence to make good choices in their own life.

Being truthful to themselves or others will make it difficult to develop a life of unwanted unacceptable habits. This allows them instead to willingly accept their role in the family and community. They will be happy and very able to choose between right or wrong.

Again it is important that your kids are aligned with family that has a constant agenda of doing good which expands their ability to stay on course.

Where there is order with a defined process to follow your kids feel more stable and see many things being done correctly. This re-enforces making good choices and keeps any disorder from their environment. We all need order in our lives to help maintain our well being. The abundance of love within a family is sure success of everyone getting along.

You must demonstrate equal time for your kids that they readily understand and experience fairness within the family. A good parent will set down expectations of what they demand from their child and reveal the consequences if they do not follow the rules.

The message needs to be that life, expectations and consequences all make sense. Making sure your kids see the correct path with proper values is how to ensure your child makes good choices.

Chapter 28: Common Pitfalls And Traps

No matter how hard people work to be terrific co-parents, there are always some communication pitfalls and traps that can catch parents by surprise. By understanding and recognizing the loopholes and possible mistakes that can happen when co-parenting, you are using one of the best ways to constantly assess your communication with the other parent. It avoids having your children getting involved in any conflict, misunderstanding or negative aspect of the divorce.

BECOMING DEFENSIVE

Keep in mind that sometimes, even when using reframes, active listening, "I" messages and focusing on the positive and collaborative aspects of the co- parenting relationship there is still the potential for finding yourself in defensive mode. Once you become defensive you are no longer willing to hear what the other person is saying and you are more focused on defending yourself with a retort or remark that you are with hearing what message is being sent, even though it may be communicated poorly.

If you find yourself becoming defensive because of what your co-parent is saying, immediately get curious about your reactions. You may have to ask for a minute to calm yourself and get back on track. This can be accomplished by simply saying "I really want to hear what you are saying and I need a minute to just consider your comments. Do you mind if we just take a short break?" During the few minutes that follow, calm down by taking a few deep breaths and thinking about what the other person said that got you in defensive mode. Identify what it was and address it so that you can put it behind you and listen when the conversation starts again. This may be a self-conversation, not out loud but in your head that sounds like:

"Ok, when I hear that same old comment about my not being on time, I get so upset.

What I need to remember is that my being late is affecting my kids, and I want to be a good parent. I accept the fact that I was late and this upset the family, so I need to listen and suggest a way to prevent this in the future. "

Becoming defensive is a natural emotional way to protect ourselves from things we don't want to hear. In some cases they may be valid, but in others they may not be accurate at all. Arguing with the other parent about what opinion is right and what is wrong is likely not to solve anything, plus it will be extremely counterproductive to the collaborative atmosphere you are trying to foster. Being right is not as important as keeping your kids out of conflict.

KIDS AS CAREGIVERS, SUPPORTERS OR MEDIATORS

Sometimes kids try to help out the parents by acting in an adult role in the communication between parents. They may also try to acts a caregiver, supporter or cheerleader for one or both of the parents. It is very important to prevent children from assuming these roles, as it can only lead to stress, anxiety and a decrease in the parent child relationship over time.

Most issues around the divorce and the parenting of children are parent issues, not open to debate, confirmation or approval of the children. Allowing children to make decision, mediate or arbitrate parent conflicts is one of the most damaging aspects of divorce. Parents need to make important life decision together, without the children, but in consideration of the children. Kids should not be asked the following questions:

- ☐ Which parent they want to live with
- ☐ How much time they want to spend with each parent
- ☐ If they want to see the other parent
- ☐ Which house they want to live in
- ☐ If they want their siblings to go with them to spend time with the other parent
- ☐ What don't they like about the other parent/ parents new partner, etc.

Kids often will try to minimize conflict by avoiding the topics they know cause angry responses by either parent. Carefully monitor what issues are not being discussed, as well as those the kids willingly bring up with you. Don't question them about why they do or don't discuss the issue, but perhaps work with the other parent to ensure that you both have a complete picture of what the kids are concerned about.

KIDS AS SPIES OR MESSENGERS

Children should not be responsible for giving messages to the other parent, or for sharing potentially unhappy news with either parent. In many cases the parent simply doesn't want to deal with the co-parents angry response to a change in plans or situations, so they have the child communicate the message. Not only does this put the child in a no win situation, but there is also an increased likelihood that the message will be relayed incorrectly or incompletely, leading to even further hostility. Consider using email or even regular mail to communicate possible high anger issues so you have time to think about what you want to say and the other parent has time to think about how they want to respond. This also keeps the kids out of the situation completely.

Kids are also sometimes used as spies to find out about financial issues, new relationships, new jobs or even new friends at a divorced parents house. Keep in mind that kids are not spies, and this really provides a moral dilemma for children. They know they are not supposed to tell the parent what information they are looking for, but they also know that lying and sneaking is wrong. If you have personal questions direct them to the other parent when the children are not present, then accept the answers and move on.

MONEY ISSUES THROUGH DIVORCE

Most families will experience a decrease in their disposable income during the divorce and for several months to years afterwards. Keeping kids as far out of the money issues caused by the divorce is important. Topics that should not be discussed or addressed in front of the children include:

- ☐ Child support amounts
- ☐ Lack of funds for basic needs for the child
- ☐ Lack of payment of child support
- ☐ Financial stress and concerns that you have as parents (bills, mortgage payments, car loan payments, etc)

What is reasonable to discuss are:
- ☐ Realistic budgets (eating out only once a month or not ordering in food all the time)
- ☐ How much allowance or spending money children will receive (in factual ways, not by blaming the other parent)
- ☐ Ensuring children that Mom and Dad have things under control with regards to finances

If finances are a concern contact a financial planner or recognized credit counseling service and work with a professional to help get on the right financial management track for the sake of the children and your peace of mind.

Chapter 29: Become A Great Stepfather

Step-parenting is hard work. Becoming a step-father has challenges all it's own. Since Father's Day is around the corner, I thought it might be nice to focus just on that role. But let's have some fun with it.

Developing a strong and healthy stepfather relationship with kids is tricky. A lot of men really don't spend a lot of time thinking about it. They're more focused on wooing their lady and assume the kid part will naturally fall into place. WRONG!!

As a Stepfather, I have given this some careful thought over the years and have devised a short list of the top 5 things to keep in mind when communicating with stepchildren:

1. It's not about you, it's about them!

Do you truly want to have a good relationship with the kids? The first thing to know is: your feelings, your wants, and your needs are simply not important to most kids.

Being a child is tough. Whatever you feel about your lot as a parent, it is a lot more challenging for the child...I promise you. When you step out there and "demand" respect, or "demand" cooperation, it just will not work!

Each person can only know their own individual reality, and this is even more true for kids; their worlds tend to be more selfish than an adult's. So just remember: try to imagine their perspective and their reality when you open your mouth! Oh, and do your best to talk "across" with them, as opposed to "down" to them!

2. Pick your battles.

My wife - bless her heart - taught me this one and it was like a mountain being lifted off of me. I began to ask myself before I complained about a towel hung incorrectly, or the folding not done right: does this really matter in the grand scheme of things?

Am I going to look back on it and say to myself: "Why did I get so caught up in such things?"

I had to project ahead and try to see the child as an adult and guess what she will say about me. What situations is she going to remember? What are the most important lessons or discussions to have with her?

Which things are more my problem than her problem? Am I sweating the small stuff? In fact, that is a good rule: "Don't sweat the small stuff...and it's mostly all small stuff."

3. Develop a special language (based in gentle love) that fits your goals.

How we say what we mean is more important than what we say. Children are much more observant than we tend to realize, and yet those perceptions can be grossly misunderstood because there might be no 'frame of reference' for the child to draw upon. So, first be sure you want to say whatever you want to say, and then be super careful about how you say it.

Is it the right timing? Is the child in a receptive frame of mind? Should you wait for a different mood or situation? Should you sit down instead of towering over the child? And, what messages do your face, eyes, and body project to the child? Uh-huh, you get the idea.

I recognize - of course - that no matter what we try, sometimes it's just not going to work. The more you try to take thoughtful care, however, the better the chances of communicating in the long run.

4. Know your outcome going in.

This is a general success concept that is commonly used in business. It is useful - if not critical - to know what your desired result is before you go in (to a meeting, or a conversation, or nearly anything else).

Map it out in your mind as much a possible: how will I react if this is said, or what do I do if this new situation develops? Try to not be caught by surprise.

Then, try to pick an 'outcome' (result) that is mutually desirable. Go in to a conversation with a goal to find a win/win result.

5. Never give up.

If youquit, you are all done. Failure is only possible when we give up; if we refuse to stop trying and we remain flexible in our approach, we can never really fail at anything.

Chapter 30: Smart Kids Are Resilient

Resilience is the ability to overcome adversity or trauma through intellectual and emotional strength. It is having confidence in one's ability to resolve difficulties; and includes the executive functions of analysis, planning, logical thinking and problem-solving.

The focus in research, as commonly seen in theories proposed by Michael Ungar and Ann Masten, has centered on two main factors – promoting well-being (i.e., Maslow's Hierarchy), and protecting against risk, or trauma. Promoting well-being and protective factors involve personal attributes of the individual, close and caring family ties, and support from the community. When these three factors – personal, family and community – are positive and healthy, then there will be a stronger resilience level than if any of these is compromised. Having a spiritual as well as a social basis for understanding can also help children cope with stress.

The American Psychological Association defines resilience as the ability to make connections with others through family ties, friendships and community support. Teaching your children to set reasonable goals, and then move toward those goals in a step-by-step manner focuses them on planning and problem-solving as well as giving them a feeling of accomplishment when they've succeeded. This, in turn, instills positive self-esteem; and helps them to see things in a broader long-term context that enables them to see past difficult times to a more optimistic future.

Changes in life are inevitable, and not everything is going to be just the way we like it. Resilience means that we're able to manage our own feelings and impulses so that we can make realistic plans and take steps to carry them out, even under duress. We can bounce back from failure, and move on with our lives. Helping our children be physically and emotionally secure gives them internal strength to be optimistic, keep things in perspective, set goals, and take decisive actions toward achieving those goals.

EXECUTIVE FUNCTION

The development of the prefrontal cortex, located in the front part of our brains, is critical for developing the emotional and cognitive capabilities required for self-regulation and what we call Executive Function – the ability to plan, concentrate, solve problems, and control our behaviors. This is also the part of our brains most affected by stress – such as a lack of safety and security in early childhood, social/emotional neglect or abuse, or poor connections to family and community support. The lack of caring and attentive parents also negatively impacts our executive functions, so developing these abilities is about smart parenting.

Executive function as defined by Harvard's Center on the Developing Child is a combination of working memory (aka, those 700 neural connections per second), selective and focused attention on important tasks (or self control), and mental flexibility — being able to revise a course of action based on changes in the environment.

As our executive function develops, we are better able to control distractions and focus on the task at hand, which means that we learn how to plan ahead and solve problems, organize information around complex tasks, use critical thinking, make good decisions and manage life stresses more productively. This also means that we're able to get along in a group and function as part of a team — essential skills for success at school and at work.

Executive function skills are essential for being able to bounce back — i.e., be resilient. These skills include being able to initiate and strategize diverse types of projects; plan and organize materials and activities to complete projects; stay on task even when obstacles arise, controlling frustrations; monitor and revise work as needed. This means having the ability to make good decisions, and then evaluate the effectiveness of those decisions to plan future activities. It requires being able to think before you act, and work through feelings of fear or frustration to reach a desired goal in a timely manner.

When this function is compromised, we have a hard time seeing the consequences of our behavior, and being flexible enough to review our plans and adapt to changing conditions. This capability can be compromised from birth, such as when infants are born to parents addicted to alcohol and/or drugs; but a sterile, unloving environment – such as in orphanages – will also damage a child's emotional self-control and critical thinking abilities. This is why a loving, nurturing environment is so essential for all children. Gaining these skills doesn't happen by osmosis – they must be learned, and learning depends upon a foundation of developmentally appropriate experiences where children can succeed, but also where they fail and learn how to deal with failure by trying again and again.

Conclusion

Raising children is hard work but it is also just about the most worthwhile work that you, I, or anyone else can possibly do. Our goal here has been not so much to give you a point by point guide to everything you need to know raise your children but to acquaint you with some of the attitudes and behaviors that I have found helpful.

Or put another way, to simply give you some basic principles that will help guide you through the tricky waters of parenthood. Figure out how to use these principles best in your own life and enjoy the greatest roller coaster ride that you will ever experience.

www.ingramcontent.com/pod-product-compliance
Lightning Source LLC
Chambersburg PA
CBHW072005070526
44583CB00015B/1342